The Waiting Game

Crisis in the organ donor system

The Waiting Game

Crisis in the organ donor system

The complete story on organ donation and transplantation

Norbert R. Hoferichter, MPA

Published in 2000 by Abbeyfield Publishers,
a division of The Abbeyfield Companies Ltd.,
33 Springbank Avenue, Toronto Ontario Canada M1N 1G2

Ordering information:
Distributed in Canada by Hushion House Distributors Ltd
36 Northline Road Toronto Ontario Canada M4B 3E2
Phone (416) 285-6100 Fax (416) 285-1777

Canadian Cataloguing in Publication Data
Hoferichter, Norbert, R., 1940–
The waiting game : the crisis in the organ donor system

ISBN 1-894584-04-X
1. Hoferichter, Norbert R., 1940– . 2. Heart–Transplantation – Patients – Canada – Biography. 3. Donation of organs, tissues, etc., – Canada. I. Title.

RD598.35.T7H63 2001   362.1'97412'0092   C00-932526-3

Editing by Bill Belfontaine
Cover and book design by Karen Petherick
Cover photo: Digital Imagery® copyright 1999 PhotoDisk, Inc.
Printing by TTP Tradeworx Ltd.

For more information visit the website: www.organtransplantbook.com.

Proceeds from the sale of this book, after production costs, will be donated to the cause of making people aware of the importance of organ donation. It is in the hope that more people will be informed and aware of this life-giving act and the inner peace it can bring to those left behind.

This book is dedicated to all those "silent heroes" who are never known to us, whom we, organ recipients, will never meet or be able to express our deepest feelings to their loved ones. These silent heroes have knowingly and selflessly given of themselves so that others may carry on enjoying life.

This book is dedicated to those individuals who had the foresight and generosity to become donors. And to their families who had the courage to see that their loved one's last will was carried out. We are very proud of you. You have given us new life and a renewed faith in mankind.

The author wishes to express
his sincere and heartfelt gratitude
to Madeline and Jim Quinn
for their support in seeing that this book became a reality.
Their twenty-year-old daughter Shara was lost to them
in a tragic car accident on December 28, 1999.
Shara was a designated organ donor,
whose last wish was never fulfilled.

Shara Quinn

Heather Ross, MD, FRCP

Heart failure is a disorder affecting more than 500,000 Canadians, contributing or causing death in 25,000 Canadians per year, and 40,000 patients are newly diagnosed each year. Congestive Heart Failure (CHF) is currently the number one reason for hospital admission and, overall, costs the healthcare system one billion dollars per year.

The overall survival rate remains 50% at five years despite significant advances in medical and surgical therapy. The overall mortality rate from CHF has doubled since 1979. The population is aging and the prevalence of CHF increases with increasing age, 1% of population over 65, 4% over age 70 to 79. Heart failure is usually inexorable, with a progressive course resulting in death. There are newer therapeutic advances being made, including heart "assist" devices, mechanical pumps that do the heart's work. However, at this time, transplantation remains the best-accepted therapy for treating end-stage heart failure. Of those people who would benefit from transplantation, only about 5%-10% are ever listed and only 75% of those will receive a transplant. This is in large part due to significant donor organ shortages.

Transplantation is the "gift of life." The joy that it brings families faced with a loved one dying is immense. Bert is such an example. He was desperately ill when he had his transplant. His was on a complicated course that required determination, will and a true fighting spirit to survive. His family never gave up hope and stood by him every step of the way. The medical team involved in his care often marvelled at his strength.

It is an honour to write the forward for his book, a book that Bert has spent a great deal of time on. It is through stories such as Bert's that we can improve donor awareness.

Assistant Professor, Division of Cardiology and Transplant
Director, Cardiac Transplant Program, The Toronto Hospital

Reg L. Perkin, MD, CCFP, FCFP, FRCPC (Hon)

I have known Bert Hoferichter for many years. We golfed together. He was the photographer for our children's weddings and our family portraits. He is a good friend.

Bert's heart problems started when he was a young man. By 1997, his heart disease had reached the point where a heart transplant was his only chance to keep on living. My wife Alison and I visited Bert and Rosemarie during the time he was on the waiting list for a heart transplant. They were both bravely facing an uncertain future.

As a physician I know what an incredible gift of life a donated organ can be to someone who has reached the end of the road with conventional treatment for a diseased vital organ. I also know the sense of satisfaction that can be experienced by the family of the donor person, knowing that a loved one's life can have a purpose beyond death. Organ donation for transplantation is a win/win proposition for society, and everything possible should be done to make it more readily available.

This book is Bert's personal story, written from the heart (no pun intended) by a very brave man who made it through death's dark vale and emerged into the sunlight on the other side. It will be tremendously helpful and supportive to patients and their families who face similar circumstances. The profits from the sale of this book will be directed towards educating the public about the value of organ donation. In my opinion, this is another win/win situation for all of us.

Dr. Reg Perkin is a well-known family physician. He is a former professor in the Faculty of Medicine at the University of Toronto and a retired executive of the College of Family Physicians of Canada.

— foreword —

Andrew J. Sarne, M.D.

I have known Bert Hoferichter for over 30 years as a friend and as his family doctor.

My comments come from my heart as I feel a deep affection for Bert having lived with him through his so-called "waiting game."

I first met him in 1967 when he was a young photographer in Port Credit and watched him become one of the most famous photographers in Canada, and the Canadian Photographer of the Year on two occasions.

In 1974, however, heart disease struck and he underwent heart bypass surgery at the Toronto Western Hospital under Dr. Baird.

In 1984 he had a heart attack. He underwent his second bypass under Dr. Tirone David in 1988.

In later years his heart deteriorated and he had to rely heavily on medications. Regular medication and naturopath treatments were tried. However as the years went by and particularly in the last two years before his transplant he became gravely disabled, unable to follow his first love, golf, as he could not walk a long distance without suffering from shortness of breath.

In 1997, after several false starts, he had a total heart transplant. But at no time did he loose faith as he looked only to the future.

Complications often follow such serious surgery but he overcame those with great strength and at this present time is back to a normal life.

I admire Bert and his family for all they have done to make people aware of the organ transplant program and this book should heighten their awareness even more.

I would like to commend him for the perseverance and the determination that he has shown in writing this book. It will help others in similar situations to have an insight and to never give up even when there appears to be no hope.

Having enjoyed good health all my life, I was little prepared for the telephone call I got from the author.

"Can we meet to discuss the publication of my book on organ donation and transplantation? It applies especially to me and to the successful heart transplantation I received a few years ago."

Ever attuned and inquisitive to delve into a topic I knew little about, I met Norbert (Bert) R. Hoferichter on a beautiful, sunny afternoon at the Boardwalk Café on Toronto's eastern waterfront. It took but a few minutes, of experiencing his vitality and enthusiasm, to become convinced that this was a social issue that was well worth airing as it had been experienced by the person who had been through it all.

I later joined Bert at a service club luncheon to learn more, see the author in action, and observe the response of the businessmen and women who comprised the audience. They were very intrigued and I could feel my enthusiasm continue to grow, wanting to get Bert's book into the hands of possible recipients, potential donors and their families, and thousands more.

This book is Bert's story, almost all the words were written by him. It is an important book that, in light of today's medical and drug research breakthroughs, has the opportunity to save many lives by spreading his knowledge and enthusiasm for the topic of organ donation and its benefits.

After a successful business and teaching career, he has made this his crusade in a life devoted to educating and encouraging the public, recipients and donors. Through many media interviews, submitted articles and speaking engagements he has encouraged hundreds to join in the life-giving donation and transplantation program that has played a major role in maintaining the lives of many thousands of people and the enjoyment of their family unit.

To publish the stories of the tragedy that befell many Donor families at the death of their loved ones, has also shown their restoration to a more peaceful acceptance of death.

Organ donation and transplantation continues to be a new dimension for me, enriching a life that has met many challenges and seen the greatness of the human spirit and the love and kindness that so many survivors exhibit.

What an honour it is to be chosen to be the publisher of this book.

V.Wm. (Bill) Belfontaine

— table of contents —

Part Two
Getting the Facts on Organ Transplantation and Donation

I wish to express my gratitude to the Toronto General Hospital's transplant team and in particular to Drs. Paul A. Daly, Heather Ross and Robert Cusimano for giving me a new life. Special thanks to Dr. Heather Ross for having encouraged me to put my thoughts on paper in the writing of this book. I also thank Dr. Vladimir Sluzar, my cardiologist for many years, for his expertise and wisdom.

I am truly thankful to my wife, Rosemarie, for having been at my bedside, day in and day out, during my 122-day stay at the Toronto General Hospital, and for fighting the "fight of all fights" with me. She lavished on me untold hours of loving care and dedication. I am also fortunate to have three wonderful children, Peter, Martin and Jackie, who suffered with me and felt my pain and agony. And I thank the Lord, who gave me the desire and willpower to survive. I believe that without my deep faith and His help, my survival would have been impossible.

Norbert R. Hoferichter

— thank you —

I am greatly indebted to the following individuals and organizations for their cooperation and help in supplying information or granting permission to use their names and stories: Madeline and Jim Quinn, all the members of HeartLinks and the Canadian Transplant Association, Maurice and Dianne Dalton, Reg and Maggie Green, Nancy and Dale Doige, Kathy Erb, Wendy Marx, executive producer of The New Health Thriveonline.com, Ken Anderson, Hillary Schieve, Donna Marie and Bryan Bowers, Sheila Hutchings, Dr. Katarina Fiala, Ron and Sue Thompson, Dr. Keith Martin, James McLaren, Dr. Jeffrey Punch, the late Dr. Andrew Lazarovits, Mr. Lou Sekora, MP, Dr. Paul Daly, Dr. Heather Ross, Eileen Young, RN, the *Toronto Star*, Reader's Digest, The Medical Post, the Canadian Institute for Health Information (CIHI), Transplant Ontario, Organ Donation Ontario, the Canadian Association for Transplantation (CAT), Health Canada, TransWeb, the United Network for Organ Sharing (UNOS), Medscape, the U.S. Department of Health and Human Services (HSS), and last but not least, all of the transplant recipients who so willingly shared their innermost feelings and personal stories with me.

My sincere thanks to my publisher, Bill Belfontaine of Abbeyfield Publishers, for believing in me and for his dedication, devotion and his endless hours of work. My deep appreciation to Kathy Lim for many hours of tireless work and her suggestions during the pre-edit of this book, and finally, my thanks to Karen Petherick of Intuitive Design for the talent to make this book and its message so compelling.

Rosemarie and Bert Hoferichter,
August 1, 1997.

Although statistics show that organ transplantation really works, unfortunately, many Canadians don't realize the extent to which organ transplants offer great new possibilities to individuals, both young and old, who are given a new lease on life and an opportunity to return to a full, active life. Nor do they realize the profound, positive impact on donor families who have been given a means to transform the loss of a loved one into a life-giving act.

This book is a timely documentation that provides easily understood information, thought-provoking discussion, personal guidance, and inspiration to transplant patients as well as to potential donors in Canada. To date, organ transplants have affected the lives of some 350,000 people worldwide.

In Canada alone, some 1,700 transplants are performed each year. This life-saving medical procedure has become the preferred method of treatment for many illnesses such as chronic kidney failure, end-stage heart disease, and liver or lung failure. The human body offers twenty-seven tissues and organs that are transplantable, any one of which can be an individual's last hope of recovery from a life-threatening condition. As a surviving transplant patient, I have learned a great deal about the process that takes place before and after a transplant operation and about the obstacles and issues the patient must face. In 1995, after a twenty-five-year battle with heart disease, my career as an award-winning photographer came to a crashing halt due to my inability to find the energy to work. In the following year I was told I had only a few more months left to live and that a heart transplant would be my last and only opportunity to survive.

My life was saved when a donor was found in February 1997 and I underwent a successful heart transplant operation at The Toronto General Hospital. Since that time I have been researching intensively into the subject of organ transplantation and have been serving as a volunteer for The Toronto Hospital, speaking publicly on the topic of organ transplantation to various organizations and diverse audiences. In February 1999, I was asked to testify before the House of Commons Health Committee as an expert on the subject of organ transplantation and give my views as they pertained to the proposed Bill M-222, a private member's bill that, if passed, would change the organ donor law in Canada.

My story as a transplant patient will help acquaint the reader with the process involved prior to and after the transplant operation—it will serve as a roadmap and a source of inspiration and guidance for patients who want to prepare for what may lie ahead. Key statistics, such as proven success and failure rates and the length of waiting lists for various transplant operations, are given. Beyond the enlightening facts and figures lies a very human approach: practical advice particular to the transplant patient is offered and the roles of the various support groups and government programs for both pre- and post-operation assistance and featured interviews with experts in the field of organ transplantation. It is an ongoing process with regards to advances in transplant medicine and related ethical issues.

The nature of the crisis in Canada's organ donor system is also addressed. What changes in organ donor law is Private Member's Bill M-222 attempting to introduce, and why are they not enough? How is Canada different from other countries such as Belgium and Austria, which enjoy a surplus in organ donation and can donate to other countries in Europe? What can Canada learn from its neighbour to the south to foster greater public awareness about the need for and the rewards involved in organ donation? What issues surround organ donation and transplantation: for example, how do the various religions in Canada view transplantation? Why is the organ donor's identity kept anonymous?

These are a few of the issues I have dealt with within the scope of this book in which I seek to dispel misconceptions about organ donation and convey to the potential donor the urgent need for their immediate concern and actions.

This book deals not only with my activities, but also with the experiences of many other Canadians. The stories attest to the great resilience and adaptability of the human body and spirit. They provide inspiration and impetus for change at a time when this country's organ donor system is in a state of crisis and transplant patients and organ donors alike must seek help in making informed decisions.

This book honours thousands of silent heroes and their families who have made it possible to bring a new life to an otherwise certain end to so many. Even if only one transplant patient or potential donor finds the comfort, hope and inner strength to carry on, I have succeeded. You are not alone; there are thousands of people who have received a new organ, and many more that are waiting in hospitals across our big nation in need of a new organ. This book will bring New Hope and joy to those who are hanging on to life by nothing more than a thin thread of hope for their unknown future. Will there be an organ for you? And if so, when? Will it arrive in time?

In Canada, approximately fourteen people in every million donate their organs: The lowest rate of organ donation per capita among the civilized countries of the world. Canada ranks at second last. How do we measure a million people? If every seat in the Toronto Skydome was filled twenty times over, it is approximately one million people. Every time you watch the Toronto Blue Jay's when the stadium is sold out, less then one individual person would donate his or her organs upon their death. Calgary, Alberta will produce approximately 12 organ donors per year.

Numerous new medications and surgical procedures are entering the field of medicine each year. Transplantation is becoming more and more the preferred method of treating end-stage illnesses such as heart, liver, kidney, lung and pancreas diseases. In Canada alone, some three hundred people die each year while on a transplant waiting list.

I would like to share my story as a surviving heart transplant patient, in the hope that it will give people faced with the prospect of undergoing an organ transplant the strength, knowledge and ability to survive and to face a new and bright future. I have written this book to show how profoundly one organ donation affects not only the organ recipient, but donor family as well—how organ donation can be the means to transform the tragic loss of a loved one into a positive, life-affirming act. It is an immense benefit to others.

Part One

Being an
Organ Transplant Patient

Family portrait taken, September 1996.

Photo by Laura MacNelly

My Twenty-Five-Year Battle
with Heart Disease

Born Under the Shadow of Heart Disease

I had known about the terrible effects of heart disease from the age of fifteen, when my father passed away of congestive heart failure. His two brothers, Fritz and Helmut, followed him shortly thereafter. My brother Hans passed away in 1999 of the same problem.

That night, on December 7, 1954, when the doorbell rang, the whole family, except for my father, was gathered in the small kitchen of our home, a small two-bedroom house in Sasbach, Germany, located at the foot of the Black Forest. Somehow faith had brought us all together that tragic evening. My twenty-nine-year-old brother Hans, my nineteen-year-old sister Lieselotte and her husband Karl, as well as my little three-year-old brother Klaus were gathered together around my mother, barely in her late forties, who sat numbly near the stove holding hands with her eighty-year-old mother, Uri. My mother was trying to prepare herself for the news she knew she was about to hear. In those days, we didn't have a telephone. All news, good or bad, was brought by the town's messenger on a bicycle. When the doorbell rang, in an instant we all knew the news we were about to receive. Father had passed away at six-thirty that evening after a long battle with heart disease. I had had a premonition all that day as I was working at a construction site high up in the Blackforest and the feeling grew stronger particularly on my way back home in the construction bus. Only a few days earlier, the doctors at the local Achener Hospital had told our family that my father's time was very limited and that at any time death could occur of congestive heart failure compounded by fluid in the lungs. He had suffered from that terrible, incurable disease for the past two years. Little was known in 1953 with regard to heart disease. Local health services would send heart patients for a two- or three-week stay to a health spa near Heidelberg; bypass surgery, diuretics or any other effective heart medication was unknown. Organ transplantation was not an item on medical research agendas in those days. With no hope for transplantation or any miracle cure or magic pill in sight, all we could hope for was that my father would be able to pass away as painlessly as possible. He was much too young to die, his life only half spent.

Before the Second World War, my father had managed to save enough money from his meager income as a carpenter to build a small home in Lauban, Schlesien. There I was born in May 1939. He had little opportunity to enjoy the fruits of his labour as during Hitler's regime he spent most of the war in the deep freezing cold of Russia, fighting people he had never known. He was one of only a handful that survived this ordeal and after the war, in 1946, my father and our family were forced to leave our home. It was no longer safe for us to stay in our little home in Schlesien. Our country's leader having started the war and lost it, we everyday citizens had to face the consequences. It was a cold and snowy day in January 1946 when my father made the decision to pack up a few of our belongings and leave his beloved home in Schlesien. Since we had a Russian officer living on the second floor of our house who kept an eye on our every move, all the preparations for our departure had to be done in complete secrecy. We packed a few of our belongings onto a small four-wheel hand cart and planned our escape for 5 a.m. the next morning. Unbeknownst to us, someone had informed the Russian officer of our plans, and when the time arrived for us to leave, he was waiting for us. All I know is that some sort of an altercation took place between him and my father, which delayed our departure by half an hour, but finally

Autumn 1945, our last family picture at home with two of our protectors, Water and Ivan (with hats on).

we were on our way. Our escorts were three Russian soldiers who were friends of my brother Hans. They were outfitted with a number of weapons, including a handheld machine gun. All three, Walter, Ivan and Pete, were what we called white Russians. They spoke perfect German and were very sympathetic to our plans for escape.

We were very fortunate to have our escorts along on this journey. After some eight hours of walking on a cold and snowy morning, we arrived at the Kohlfort railstation without further incident. The snipers and partisans along the route must have had respect for our Russian friends, for no shots were fired. At the station we were all body searched, a tradition of the occupying forces. Being the youngest in our family of twelve, my job was to carry and guard whatever family heirlooms we were able to take with us. I was carrying all our valuable family documents, all our photographs and a few pieces of jewelry and other knickknacks in a small school rucksack—a good hiding place, I thought. Luckily, since I was only six years old, the Russians left me alone. The incident with my father and the Russian officer as well as the poor weather that morning delayed our arrival at the train station by one hour and we missed the scheduled train. Perhaps it had been a blessing in disguise. Despite the war being officially over, terrorist activities were still taking place on both sides. The train that we were trying to catch that morning was bombed and derailed and a great number of people lost their lives. After a number of stops in various camps on our way north to get food and shelter, the women, including my sister, were deloused, and we arrived safely in Whilhelmshaven, Ostfriesland.

We officially became displaced persons, or DPs, in our own country, wandering through various camps and makeshift hostels. After a short-lived stay in the very north of Germany, in Ostfriesland, we made the decision to move our family to a beautiful new land called Baden, in the heart of Germany's Black Forest. We arrived there after a two-day train trip with only our personal belongings. We had just enough worldly belongings to carry onto the train and that was how we had arrived at the little village of Sasbach to start a new life.

Father started to build a home for the second time in his life. The town had donated a plot of land to us, and with the sweat and hard labour of every member of our family, we built a small but cozy two-bedroom home. It was my father's pride and joy after bringing his entire family safely through those six horrible war years. But only three years later, at the age of forty-six, the joy and pleasure of his new found land and his new home was taken from him.

Construction of our new home in 1950, Sasbach in the Blackforest.

Heart disease had taken the lives of my father's two brothers, who had died before the age of sixty, as well as that of my beloved brother Hans, who had been not only a brother to me, but a surrogate father and a good friend as well. Having suffered from the symptoms of heart disease from the age of forty-five, Hans passed away in February 1999 from an aneurysm of the aorta at age seventy, making him the longest-living Hoferichter dating back to the 1860s. Even so, his death was a hard blow for me, having just received a new heart with a new lease on life.

But growing up as a child, I was blissfully unaware that I was genetically programmed to inherit my father's heart problems, that I was a walking time bomb ready to explode. I was not prepared for what I was about to undergo because of this hereditary disease. The year my father died, I had finished my basic eight years of public schooling and had wanted to eventually go on to university, but my family could not afford to send me to high school, let alone university. With the main breadwinner now gone, we all had to work to provide the family income. Education was not free. Strangely, white-collar work was frowned upon by our family; as a family of blue-collar workers, this was the only way, in my parents' eyes, to earn an honest living. Unwillingly, yet dutifully, I entered an apprenticeship to become a stonemason and bricklayer. It was one profession that was much in

Richard Gauss and I Christmas 1957, completing our immigration documents for Canada.

demand at the time. Germany had to be rebuilt. Those were very hard years for me, as I had to help support my mother as well as myself.

In April 1957 I finished my three-year apprenticeship to become a qualified bricklayer, but I was yearning to see more of the world. Against the wishes of my mother, but with the blessing of the rest of the family, my friend Richard and I immigrated to Toronto, Canada, a place we had selected without much research. We had no relatives to greet us once we arrived or to offer support in time of need. On May 24, 1958, just seven days after my eighteenth birthday, we embarked on the *New York*, an ocean liner from the Greek Line that was on her way to New York via Halifax. Richard and I were both eighteen years of age when we arrived from Halifax after a three-day train trip. Somehow, we expected that someone would be greeting us as we arrived at the Toronto Union railway station that rainy morning. But there was to be no such luck. There we were in our newly chosen country with less than twenty dollars in our pockets with no place to go and no one to lean on for help. Through a young immigrant we met from Germany, we found a room in downtown Toronto, at the Central YMCA on College Street.

We had eight dollars between the two of us to last a week. My knowing very little English continued to plague me. I remember the day after our first shopping trip, we had gotten just a few essentials such as toothpaste and razor blades. I rushed into the washroom at the YMCA to brush my teeth. My first thought was, what an awful-tasting toothpaste they have in this country—only to discover that I was using "Brylcream" that was meant for my hair. There were few immigration services or places that one could turn to for help in those days. For the occasional free board or meal, one could find a church somewhere that would lend a helping hand. But was there no one who could or would help us in this new and wonderful country? My friend and I had little or no knowledge of the English language and knew even less about the North American way of life. We faced quite a challenge in those early days, and it was very hard to make a completely new start in a country whose language and customs were totally unfamiliar to us. We arrived in Canada at a time that was not hospitable to European immigrants. With very few exceptions, the only immigrants permitted came from Italy, Germany and Great Britain. The country had few job opportunities and those that were available were earmarked for anglophones or Canadian citizens only. I remember applying for a job at the Toronto Transit Commission and their first question was, "Are you a British subject or a Canadian citizen?" The answer, of course, was no. "Sorry, but these jobs are reserved for British subjects and Canadian citizens," was their reply.

The very country that opened its doors to you slammed them right back in your face. Most advertisements in the newspaper for jobs, no matter how unimportant they might be, would only hire Canadian citizens or people from Britain. This was particularly true of jobs with the municipal, provincial or federal government. We accepted the situation; these were the laws and rules of the country we had chosen, and we respected that. Were we offended, did we riot or burn down government buildings? No, of course not; we just looked elsewhere for work. For us immigrants, it was a decade where we found very little assistance being offered from the government. Only determination and very hard work could bring us success. It was hard in those first years. It would have been easier to turn around and go back to my family in Germany, but pride and the will to succeed kept me in my new country. Despite the setbacks and adjustments that had to be made, there was something about this new way of life that appealed to me. I had left a small town in the middle of the Black Forest, protected by my family. All of a sudden I was on my own, independent, forced to rely on my own resourcefulness without outside interference or help.

At the age of nineteen, heart disease was the least of my concerns. Occasionally, the thought of my father's early demise crept into my mind. Why had he died so young? Was there a family history of heart disease? My mother and older brother had confirmed that other family members and relatives had died of the same disease. But having found this out, I had given the matter little thought and was busy getting on with my life. I was more worried about making enough money to pay for my room and board or being able to buy streetcar tickets to get to work. If I ran short of money, I could always rely on a bit of help from my good friend Richard, who at that stage had a well-paying job as a barber. Meanwhile, I had found a factory job that paid a grand total of thirty dollars a week for fifty-five hours of work. It was enough money to pay for my room and board, buy streetcar tickets and sometimes send ten dollars home to my mother in Germany. I was happy in my new job, where I was among German-speaking people with whom I could exchange ideas and dreams about this new and wonderful country that we had chosen.

Sunshine entered my rather bleak life on the Monday morning of September 12, 1959. I met the woman who was about to change my life, another German immigrant, who had landed in Canada with her parents just a month prior to my arrival. I was given the opportunity to meet the newly-hired office girl by the name of Rosemarie Stennull, who was to seal envelopes for fifty cents an hour. I found out later that it was a blatant set-up by the owner of the business. He must have known that I needed companionship very desperately. In my eyes, she was a good-looking seventeen-year-old. It was not love at first sight, but she was a great companion, with qualities that made her different from most other girls I had known. We became good friends and grew very fond of each other over the ensuing months and years. Against the will of her parents, we announced our wedding plans, choosing April 13, 1963, as our wedding day. We purchased our first home, a three-bedroom bungalow built on a ravine lot. We thought we were in heaven. A year later our first son, Peter, was born. This prompted my employer to give me a generous salary increase of five dollars a week. Rosemarie stopped working and became a full-time mom. In order to maintain prompt mortgage payments, I decided to work at night and on weekends for a bakery cleaning baking sheets.

In 1962 I made photography, my longtime hobby, a full-time profession and my true life's work. I was never cut out to be a manual labourer or sit in an office eight hours a day. At the early age of thirteen, I had understood cameras and their processes, and I took real pleasure in photographing my brother Hans's wedding. I knew I had what it would take to be a good photographer as it came naturally to me. I needed a more creative outlet and photography afforded me that. For the next five years I freelanced, but only on a part-time basis. My work became published in major Toronto newspapers, such as the *Toronto Star*, *The Telegram* and the *Globe and Mail*, as well as a number of magazines. I was selling photos, and writing stories that were typed by a loyal secretary at the company that I was working for. I soon made more money from my photography than from my full-time job. Despite my wife's misgivings, I decided to sell our first home.

With the profit we realized on the sale of our home, I purchased my first studio in 1967, and soon expanded to three studios and photo retail stores. In 1970, and again in 1971, I was presented with the highest honour in my profession in Canada, the Canadian Professional Photographer of the Year Award, which is given to only one working photographer each year. It was presented to me in Niagara Falls at the National Convention of the Professional Photographers of Canada by none other than my lifelong idol, Yousuf Karsh. I was honoured, and felt that I had arrived, that I was a somebody.

Receiving my first, "Canadian Professional Photographer of The Year Award" presented by world famous portrait photographer, Yousuf Karsh, 1970.

I went on to win the award again in the following year and collected thirty-five more national and international awards for my work. At the age of thirty-one I received my master's degree in photographic arts from the Professional Photographers Association in Canada as well as in the United States. I went on to host my own TV show, write a newspaper column on photography, and be in demand as a seminar and convention speaker, even appearing on national TV talk shows. I had found success, but with it had come increasing stress and pressures, and my health started to suffer. My brain and my feet were working faster than my heart would allow. I was burning the candle at both ends. Something had to give.

At my favourite place to relax, the Mississaugua Golf Club, I found some relief from the strain of my daily activities. But it was not enough. I had my first heart attack, and a series of bypass operations and other health-related problems ensued. After a twenty-five-year battle with heart disease, my health had taken a turn for the worse. By the recommendation of Dr. Vladimir Sluzar, I went to see Dr. Paul

Daly at the Toronto Hospital's heart transplant division. Dr. Daly felt that the longer we waited, the better my chances would be. I continued to see Dr. Daly two or three times each year and in August 1996 I was finally told that my only chance for prolonging my life was an organ transplant. I was placed on a waiting list for a heart to be donated by a complete stranger, at a time I couldn't foretell, left only to hope that it would occur as soon as possible.

My First Heart Attack and the Next Two Decades

The day had begun innocently enough. It was a beautiful morning in the spring of 1974, and my family had just opened our in-ground swimming pool. I had returned just the day before, from a long photographic assignment and was horsing around with my children in the backyard pool of our gorgeous home in Lorne Park Estates, just west of Toronto. Suddenly, the pain hit me like a thirty-ton truck and stopped me cold. I recovered quickly. I didn't mention the incident to my wife or to anyone else, thinking it would not happen again.

The next Monday I started a major photographic assignment for Ontario Place in Toronto—a twelve-week shoot, spread throughout the four seasons of the year. On my way back home that month, after working for three weeks in northern Ontario, the pain hit me again. I was getting on a plane, carrying my equipment up the boarding ramp. As I sat down, I felt this tremendous pain in my chest and down my left arm. It was very scary. It took some twenty minutes before the pain in my chest and left arm finally subsided. Upon landing in Toronto I phoned Rosemarie from the airport to have her set up an immediate appointment with my family doctor. His diagnosis was not what I had expected it to be. He told me that I had heartburn and to not worry about it. I knew very well that this was not the case.

I insisted on seeing a cardiologist the next week. I asked the doctor to have me perform a two-step test, one that had me climbing stairs and doing other strenuous activities. Although I was perfectly fine as long as I wasn't exerting myself physically, that test did indeed show problems. My cardiologist recommended an angiogram. I had to wait another three months. It confirmed that I had a severe blockage of the coronary arteries. I was thirty-four at the time.

The surgeons suggested that a triple bypass operation be performed within a week. But my family and I had already planned our two-week holiday to Canada's East Coast and nothing was about to stop me from going. It was not a wise decision. On that trip, I climbed down a steep embankment in order to get just the right angle for a photograph, but returning to the top, about halfway up the slope, I felt the same severe pain as before in my chest and left arm. With a long rest, some nitroglycerin, and the help of my wife and three children, I finally made it back up the embankment, but that rather frightening incident put a damper on the rest of our vacation.

Six months later, in October 1974, I was admitted into Toronto Western Hospital for triple bypass surgery, which was still a somewhat new and risky procedure in those days. The operation was a success and I was able to leave the hospital after a two-week stay and after a further five-day recovery period in a rehabilitation home. I was finally ready to go home, and I resumed work six weeks later. I felt great and everything looked very promising.

The first item on my to-do list was to complete the assignment for Ontario Place that I had started two months earlier. Some other major photographic projects lay ahead, including one that would test the extent of my recovery the most, the twenty-first Olympic Games in Montreal. I was hired by COJO, the official organization in charge of recording and broadcasting the Games. All went well with that assignment, and it was a gratifying job that I would not have missed for all the money in the world.

My business continued to flourish and I was in demand for my photographic abilities. Over the following ten years, between October 1974 and December 1984, I led a full life. I often knew that I was burning both ends of the candle, but it was difficult to turn down the rewarding professional opportunities that came my way.

But close to ten years after my first bypass operation, I began to feel my energy level deteriorating, and I again began experiencing chest pains. In December 1984, I had my first post-operation heart attack, in the parking lot of the Mississaugua Golf Club. It was my year as president of the Port Credit Rotary Club and it had also been a very busy season in my photographic career.

I sat in my car, knowing that I was going through a heart attack. All the symptoms were there, but I didn't have enough sense to call an ambulance. I just drove myself home. Rosemarie was out at a ladies' meeting, so I went to bed, hoping the chest and arm pains would go away. Later that evening, when the pain did not subside, I had one of my children call for an ambulance. The next ten days were spent in the hospital. I treated that episode as a serious warning, but resumed my work after a few weeks.

In June 1987 I had a second angiogram and it showed new blockages of the coronary artery. The original bypass had lasted fourteen years. I was further diagnosed with an aneurysm on the aorta that could burst at any moment. After many consultations with my cardiologist, Dr. Vladimir Sluzar, and Dr. Tirone David at Toronto Western Hospital, the decision was made to operate to try to fix the blockages and stabilize the aneurysm.

In December of 1988, Dr. David performed the second bypass operation and added a screening around the ballooned aneurysm. The night before the operation, Dr. David came to see me in my hospital room, just to talk. He made it clear that it was a dangerous operation and that I had a one-in-four chance of survival, odds that were not to my liking. I was very worried. But I was only forty-nine years of age, had three young children, a successful career and many reasons for living. I had absolute trust in Dr. David and unswerving faith in the Lord. I told the doctor to do his best and One much higher up would take care of the rest. The operation went well, but I never felt quite right afterwards. My endurance and aerobic capacity were rather limited. I knew that I was not yet out of the woods.

In December of the following year, with little warning I suffered massive hemorrhaging. My nose and eyes started overflowing with blood. It was more than just a nosebleed. The bleeding was unstoppable. My son Martin drove me to the hospital emergency room, and I was rushed into the operating room. I spent Christmas of that year in the hospital away from my family with a badly bruised and bandaged face. The hemorrhaging, it turned out, had resulted from having taken too many blood-thinning drugs. Over the next three years I underwent monthly blood tests and the first discussion of a possible heart transplant came up.

In January 1992 I saw Dr. Sluzar—the fine young cardiologist who had long been taking care of me, and whose advice, wisdom and expertise I had come to respect and trust. It was his opinion that some time down the road I should consider a heart transplant. "But let's not rush into it. The longer we wait, the better the outcome will be." I kept hearing those words from Dr. Sluzar repeating over and over again in my mind. That possibility offered a very faint glimmer of hope in what had otherwise seemed a hopeless world for me. I knew that my body would not be able to tolerate for much longer the amount of drugs I was taking. I underwent several stress tests and every conceivable heart test devised, and we came to the conclusion that a heart transplant would be the only answer. My system was slowly shutting down; I was having problems with my kidneys and pancreas as well as with my lungs.

I went to have a series of tests done by Dr. Paul Daly, the heart transplant coordinator at Toronto Hospital—and after numerous tests, Dr. Daly felt that it was still premature for me to undergo a heart transplant. His comment, similar to that of Dr. Sluzar, was that "the longer we wait, the more we have to gain from advances in medication and technology." It was my first contact with Dr. Daly and with the Toronto Hospital.

In March 1994 I went to Florida searching for a second opinion. I combined my winter holiday with a visit with Dr. Gene E. Myers, a renowned cardiologist in Sarasota, Florida. His opinion was somewhat different from that of my Canadian doctors. He suggested an operation would be able to cure my problem. But back in Toronto Dr. Sluzar felt that it was too risky and I agreed with him.

In 1985, I had decided to sell my studios after I was offered a position as department head of creative photography at Humber College in Toronto. It was both a blessing and a challenge for me, and the changes made to the department under my new leadership were applauded by the photo industry. Meanwhile, I went to see Dr. Daly as well as Dr. Sluzar every six months. My condition was tolerable and I felt less stress in my new job than when I had been self-employed. But teaching is not as easy as it is often made out to be. The stress took a further toll on my health and my heart was not able to hold up under the strain of my daily life. By May 1995 my condition was becoming more serious by the day and I gave up my position as department head to become an active instructor. The pressure would be somewhat less than before, and that, I hoped, would help me to stay active in my work. But in the middle of that month, I had to go back to the hospital. I had a very low heart beat and I felt terrible. While waiting for a room in the emergency ward, I was put onto an audible heart monitor. I could tell that my heart rate was down to about twenty-two beats per minute. Once in a while, my heart would stop beating altogether. The first time that happened, a horde of nurses rushed to my bedside, checking to see whether I was still alive. To avoid that from happening again, I pounded my chest every time the beat went quiet on the audible monitor.

I later found out that due to a misunderstanding about the required dosage for the drug Dioxin, I had overdosed to a point where my blood count showed a dioxin level of 8.0. A normal level would have been around 0.8.

For the following four days I was spaced out. I didn't know where I was or even who I was, and it was a very hard time for my family. During that time, I had a number of frightening hallucinations and spoke only in German—something I seldom did. Oh, those drugs can play some pretty funny tricks on your mind. I remember being asked by a nurse, "Mr. Hoferichter, tell me where you are," and my answer being "Can't you see I'm driving my bed right down Yonge Street, but the traffic is killing me?" After seven days the dioxin level in my blood returned to normal and I went home. But it had been a very close call. I was still working as a full-time instructor at Humber College at the time, but the possibility of an early retirement loomed before me as the weeks went by. Four months after that episode, back I went to the hospital, this time because my heart was showing an irregular heart rhythm. After a change of medication during a five-day stay, the problem was corrected and I went home once more. But finally, the day I most feared came later that same month—the day I had to retire from my teaching profession at Humber College. I could no longer carry on. Even the students kept asking me what was wrong with me: why was I so blue in the face and in the ears? Actually, it was from lack of oxygen resulting from poor circulation, my heart was just too weak to continue pumping enough blood throughout my body and I was always cold no matter what the temperature. I just could not face the questions my students kept asking. They were great students but I did not want to share my health problems with them. The decision to retire from my job, which I really loved, was a very hard one to reach. But there was no other choice. My standards of professionalism and teaching were too high to let me do only a half-hearted job. I bade a sad farewell to the college, and to photography, the profession I loved.

My wife and I felt that a few months of sunshine would do us a world of good and we went to Florida sometime in January of the following year. Little did I realize how really ill I had become. The mind plays strange games, I was unaware that the end might be near. My wife, my children and all the activities I was engaged in, kept me quite busy and I had little time to sit down and worry about my illness. This was no doubt a blessing; at times the process of deteriorating health can be sped up by too much worry.

During that time, despite great doses of diuretics, I retained a tremendous amount of fluid in my lungs and the rest of my body. My weight ballooned up from about 140 pounds to 170 pounds, and my waist size expanded from a size 32 to 38. I was not a happy camper. I saw a doctor in Fort Myers, and with his help, the use of a new diuretic, plus lots of rest with my legs up, the fluid level came down. In one month I lost about thirty pounds of fluid. My only concern was what those drugs were doing to my liver and kidneys. By then my energy level was just about zero and I avoided even the shortest walk around the block. All I wanted to do was to sit in the hot Florida sun and try to keep myself warm.

Making my way back to Toronto was very difficult for me. Thinking back now, I could have died right then and there. The new diuretic and all the other pills made me very ill and weak, and Rosemarie did most of the driving while I tried to put on a good face. We planned the trip back in such a way that we would always be in reach of a hospital and every hour we stopped so I could use a washroom. I can only thank God that we were able to make it back. Upon our arrival home, I immediately went to see Dr. Sluzar. Further blood tests confirmed that besides my weak heart, my kidneys were not functioning well, the creatine level in my body was way up and my liver was not in the best of shape. It was high time to speak to Dr. Daly of Toronto Hospital's heart transplant team again.

In July 1996 Dr. Daly and Dr. Sluzar reached the decision to put me on the heart transplant waiting list. I was now one of many. I remember how Dr. Daly looked at the names on the waiting list after my question as to how many were ahead of me. All I saw were reams of names. I was told the waiting time could be anywhere from a few weeks to a year and that it would depend largely on the availability and suitability of the donor. The severity of my condition was such that I reached the top of the priority list within seven months.

Before the actual transplant operation, the hospital tried to lower my body's fluid level by putting me on a restricted fluid diet. It was a must for the upcoming transplant operation to be successful. But all the diuretics in the world could not help me anymore, as my kidneys and my whole body had built up a tolerance to all the drugs I had been taking over the past ten years. For a week I lay in the hospital bed with wires and conductors coming out of every opening and vein in my body, hoping to lose more fluid. When I got home I stepped on my scale, and guess what? I had not lost an ounce. I didn't have the heart to tell Dr. Sluzar that the procedure hadn't worked. He had really tried for me, but now my body was tired and would no longer cooperate.

My condition continued to deteriorate by the day, and even the smallest task became a major burden to me. In the cold November and December months, the heating in our home was kept on at full blast, and in addition to the regular heating we had a large wood-burning fireplace. I lived on top and in front of the stove every day. In my bed at night, I would take an old-fashioned bottle warmer to keep my feet warm. I had little circulation left in my system and the cold winter weather was my constant enemy.

The time had come to face up to reality. For the first time in my twenty-five-year struggle with heart disease, I felt that the end might be near. Yet I remained full of hope, knowing that my destiny was in the hands of God. I was so grateful to see the sun rise every morning and be able to spend another pleasant day with my loving wife and children.

But there was one black cloud that had been hanging over me for many years, one that I simply had not been able to shake off. In my younger days I had not been faithful. This had been gnawing at me tremendously and I was sure that I was now being punished for my mistakes. I was absolutely convinced that I had to make peace with the Lord and ask my wife for forgiveness before undergoing what lay ahead of me. I had been in a profession that had me away for weeks on end, conducting seminars on photographic assignments; temptation had been ever present. But I knew I could not leave this earth or make a new beginning without clearing my conscience and asking for forgiveness. I just had to level with my beloved wife and with the Lord. Tears streaming down her face, she forgave me.

—•—

I received a phone call early on the morning of January 9, 1997, from Dr. Sluzar, who was at the airport, ready to depart on his family holidays. Before he left, he wanted to make sure that I saw Dr. Daly, the transplant coordinator at Toronto Hospital, as soon as possible, as he had just examined the results of blood test done earlier that week.

The results were not very good. Dr. Daly had me admitted immediately to the Toronto Hospital. The waiting game for a new heart and the promise of a new start to life had begun.

On the Transplant Waiting List

Not every organ transplant case progresses the way mine did; there are seldom two cases that follow the same pattern. The length of the waiting list and the post-operation stay and care depend entirely on the type of organ being transplanted. It can take up to three years to receive a kidney for transplant and as little as six days for a heart. Each case is evaluated and assessed by a team of transplant doctors. Bryan Pratico of Vernon, BC, whose fifteen-month-old daughter received a new heart at The Toronto Hospital for Sick Children on Christmas Day 1999, said, "Our daughter got her new heart in six days and that is big news. Wouldn't it be great if everyone got it that quick? It could happen if everyone was a donor. There would be no waiting period for babies of up to a year, there would be no one needlessly dying at such a very young age because of lack of donors."

Unfortunately, the Pratico case is a very rare occurrence. The facts speak for themselves. In 1999, fifteen young people died at The Toronto Hospital for Sick Children while waiting for an organ transplant. With Canada's very low organ donor rate, we have a very long way to go in order to achieve this goal.

When in June 1996 Dr. Daly decided that it was time for me to undergo a number of tests to make sure that a prospective new heart would find a good and suitable home in me, I was told that the donor could be male or female. Race or colour made no difference, as long as the blood and tissue type were a match with mine. The donor had to be approximately my size and weight for the new heart to fit into my chest cavity. After a number of blood tests as well as tests for HIV infection were carried out and the condition of my kidneys, liver, lungs and other vital organs were found in working order, a decision was reached to put me on the transplant waiting list.

Once on the list, my emotional outlook started to change. I had renewed hopes and I was looking forward to a full and active life. It was a great relief knowing that perhaps someday I would receive an opportunity to restart my life. I had always been an active person, but in the last few years I felt as if someone had cut my legs out from under me. It had been difficult for me to see people walking by my house on their way to a golf game or off to a skiing party at Blue Mountain in Collingwood. Activities that only a few years ago had been part of my daily life had become only a pleasant, sometimes frustrating memory, and watching others lead an active life that I could not participate in had been very disheartening to me. In those last days before the operation, much of my time was spent watching TV and reading books, and quite often I would be overcome with emotion and tears would roll down my face. At the age of only fifty-seven, I didn't want my life to be taken away from me. But most of the time I forced myself to be in a very positive frame of mind. I could see the light at the end of the tunnel. I kept reaching for it, knowing there was sunshine ahead, praying that I would arrive there in time.

Being placed on the waiting list was much like being caged like a bird. A personal pager was my twenty-four-hour companion for the next six months, courtesy of the Bell Telephone Company. I also had a car phone, as well as a packed suitcase that travelled with me at all times outside the house, even if I was only going to the local grocery store or church service. Living one hundred and forty kilometres north of the organ transplant hospital presented its own unique problems, but Dr. Daly was always reassuring and he felt that the distance would not be a major problem. The time frame from acquiring the heart from the donor to the actual beginning of the transplant was about six to eight hours. If there was a severe snowstorm or other unforeseen weather-related circumstance that would make it difficult to arrive at the hospital within the allotted time frame, an emergency helicopter would be provided for me.

Days and weeks went by, but no call came from the hospital. A number of times my personal pager went off in the middle of the night, but these were mainly false alarms. Each time the exhausted but still pumping heart inside me felt like it was jumping out of my throat. Even a simple ringing of the telephone would send shivers up and down my spine. After a while I got used to it. It was important to answer the call, no matter if it was a false alarm or not. It could also be a test. All my movements were very restricted. Whether we went out to visit someone or to take in an evening at the symphony, I was always mindful that a call could come at any time without warning. I had to be prepared, know the shortest route to the hospital and be on my way at a moment's notice.

My seven months on the waiting list seemed like an eternity. It was an anxious time for me, knowing that at any moment the little power that was left in my heart, the one organ that had connected me emotionally and physically to my parents and heritage, could flicker and die away. After all, beyond the physical, there is also the emotional, cultural significance attached to the heart. From the time we are children we are told to always act from a good heart. And in songs, poems, in all of literature, the heart is praised and alluded to as the seat of human emotion. Just think, how many love songs are there that mention a person's heart? Meanwhile, questions such as, "Will I be the same person after the transplant?" "Will my emotional and spiritual outlook change?" or, "Will I act differently than before?" kept creeping into my mind. I had many misgivings but kept them to myself. It is so difficult to put these feelings into words; only someone who has gone through this traumatic medical miracle can really understand my thoughts.

I continued to see Dr. Daly as well as my own cardiologist, Dr. Sluzar, on a regular basis. On January 9, 1997, I received a phone call to see Dr. Daly again. After a number of blood tests, the results of which were not favourable, the decision was made to admit me into the hospital. Little did I know what lay ahead of me. For the third time my chest would be opened from top to bottom, and again I would spend many days in the intensive care unit. But I had confidence in the Lord and in the physicians around me. What I did not know at the time was that for next five months, the hospital would become my home away from home. I would be undergoing four major operations and I would come so very close to dying. Even my doctors had little hope for my survival.

As I was waiting in the hospital for my new heart, the thought that kept going through my mind was, how ironic this whole thing was. Here I am, with little more than a great deal of hope, waiting for someone else to give up his or her life for me to carry on. I kept watching the nightly TV news and hoping for bad weather. Surely, I kept thinking, there must be an accident happening somewhere that would produce the right heart donor for me. Or perhaps somewhere there might be a tragedy unfolding and among the casualties would be organ donors. If this sounds barbaric or selfish, you're absolutely right.

But it is hard to pass judgment on someone unless you've been in the exact same circumstances as them.

The number one priority for the next four weeks was to reduce my fluid levels. Because my heart had had little strength to supply blood to my bodily organs over the past few months, the rest of my vital organs, such as my liver, lungs and kidneys, were not functioning properly, and because of that my body had filled with excess fluid. I was put on a fluid-restricted diet, which was more stringent than I could have ever imagined. For the next four weeks I was allowed three thimblefuls (one fluid ounce) of ice water each day. It was sheer torture. Being in a small room that was hot and dry, my craving for fluid became a full-time preoccupation. I lost fifteen pounds in body fluid in those weeks, enough for a new heart to be able to function without danger of being overloaded. Going to the bathroom was virtually impossible. With the lack of fluid in my system, on top of a regular diet of solid food, every bowel movement sounded like large rocks falling on a tin roof. My stomach felt like a cement mixer with too little water. But I had great nurses who felt sorry for me. Every evening, when it got quiet in the ward, they would sneak a Popsicle into my room. It was like Christmas all over again. I became absolutely Popsicle-addicted. In fact, whenever I dreamt, it was quite often about Popsicles. I would dream of seeing cases of Popsicles next to my bed and would instruct my wife to make sure the fridge was full of them when I got home. Drugs can play funny tricks on your mind.

The Operation

By February 5, 1997, one month had passed since my entry to the hospital. Two hearts had been available to me, but unfortunately they were not acceptable according to the doctors. I was told in advance by the medical staff that false alarms could and would happen. The first heart had been from a donor with diabetes, and the other available heart had been from an HIV or hepatitis patient. The doctors had turned both of these down. The match had to be perfect. At four-thirty that afternoon, I was introduced for the very first time to my new granddaughter, Katherine, born to my daughter Jackie and her husband Kevin. With special permission from the head nurse, my daughter was able to bring Katherine to my bedside. What a joy it was for me to see her; but our first meeting could not have been under more difficult circumstances. Katherine joined me in my hospital bed. She was carefully placed on my chest to avoid disturbing all the electrical leads and tubes that were attached to my body, and at that moment I broke out into an uncontrollable stream of tears. I held her for a few minutes. Would this be our first, and perhaps last, meeting, or would I be able to see her grow up, take her on long walks and enjoy her company? Only the Lord could answer these questions. It was great to see Katherine; I received an inner peace knowing that I had met her. After the family left, I felt an even more urgent desire to survive the upcoming operation. There was so much to live for, I can't have my life end now, I thought to myself.

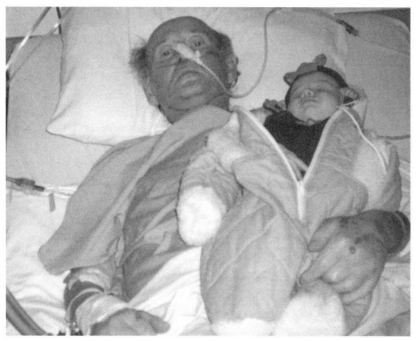

My first grand-daughter, Katherine, one hour before my transplant.

Late that afternoon, after the others had left, Rosemarie was at my bedside and we were absorbed in a game of cards. All at once my room started to fill up with a number of doctors and nurses. What a beehive of activity! I knew that it was "show-time." I was told that a suitable heart had been located and that there was a strong possibility of receiving a transplant that evening. The ensuing events in my room were much like what I had thought it must be like when being prepared for an execution. Last-minute tests and medication were given to me to calm me down, I was shaven and bathed, and given a few minutes of time to be alone with my wife and say our last prayers together. The waiting game was finally over. I was ready, having made peace with the Lord and having kissed Rosemarie good-bye. I remember my last words, "Let's go and do it."

My fate was always in the hands of the Lord and now it also rested with my surgeons. By eight o'clock that night I had entered the operating room at the Toronto Hospital, which I was not to leave until two-thirty the next morning. Rosemarie, who at the time was staying with my daughter in Toronto, was told to go home and get some sleep as there was little she could do except wait and pray. At two-thirty the next morning, her phone rang and Dr. Cusimano told my wife, to her great relief, that the operation had been a success. He mentioned that the old heart had been in much worse condition than he had thought. The operation had lasted six hours because of excessive bleeding. But Dr. Cusimano was extremely happy with the new heart that I had received.

That year, Transplant Ontario's waiting list contained 829 people waiting for a new kidney, 134 for a new liver, 31 for a heart transplant, 29 for a lung transplant and 6 people for a heart and lung transplant, which brought the number of organs needed that year to 1,029 in Ontario alone. I was one of the truly fortunate people who had received a new heart in time.

Three days into my recovery, Rosemarie had her first conversation with me. I was well sedated and unable to communicate. The next ten days were spent in intensive care, somewhat longer than in most cases, and I suffered from a collapsed lung and was still constipated. None of those factors were helping to speed up my recovery.

After the operation, the new heart worked fine. But shortly thereafter, further complications and difficulties began to emerge. I underwent three more operations that had to do with my stomach and with fluid retention in my lungs. Dr. Sonnenberg removed about one and a half litres of fluid from my lungs by inserting a syringe into my lower back and drawing out as much fluid as possible. This helped a bit in alleviating the problem with my breathing and my lungs, but it was not completely resolved.

By February 21, sixteen days after the operation, I was terribly constipated, having not had a bowel movement for some weeks. Although I was no longer on a fluid-restricted diet, I was unable to go to the washroom. I had been experiencing severe pain in my stomach for the past week, and all attempts to move my bowels had failed. I must have had ten enemas and taken every possible oral medication. Nothing worked. Finally, Dr. Sonnenberg decided that something had to be done, and he loosened the stool by inserting his fingers and removing it manually. It was a very painful process. For three weeks I had been completely constipated, and my doctors feared that my intestines had burst. I went back into the operating room for exploratory surgery. I began to contemplate suicide, wondering when the pain would finally stop.

Drs. Ross and Sonnenberg at my bedside.

I was ready to put an end to it all myself. I felt I couldn't stand the pain any longer, I couldn't stand having all those needles stuck into me every day. I felt as if didn't have the strength or will to go on, that I'd reached absolute rock bottom. I'd had enough. I wrote a note to my wife and family explaining why I was ending my own life, wishing them all the best in the future. I was only sorry that I would not be able to see Katherine grow up and be a companion as well as a loving grandfather to her.

My thoughts about ending my life that night has become a dream that haunts me time and time again. In the dream, the doctors smiled as they assist me in my suicide, and I see them bending over me and giving the fatal dose of poison. "Don't worry, it will take two days before you die," they assure me. I fall into a deep sleep and my dream begins. It takes place in a beautiful, lush green meadow with thousands of gorgeous flowers and clean blue streams running right through the middle of the meadow. It is unbelievably beautiful, but I don't have my camera with me. A terrible fear overcomes me. I scream at the doctors, "Please stop, I don't want to go, I have so much more beauty on this earth to record. Please give me time, I'd like to change my mind." But all I see is the solemn faces of the doctors in white coats shaking their heads, meaning, no, sorry, it's too late. I would usually wake up from this dream in a cold sweat and with a loud scream. But I am so grateful to this day that it is only a dream.

But my suicide attempt is not unusual. Talking with so many transplant patients over the past years, I was amazed to learn how many others had had similar thoughts and experiences. At the time, all sorts of ideas as to how to end my life had entered my mind: starving to death, suffocating myself, jumping out of the window or just running away from it all. In hindsight, I realize it would have been very difficult for me to try to end it all in my hospital bed without any kind of outside assistance. But I later realized that bowing out at that time would have been cowardly and selfish, I couldn't do that to my family and to all these doctors who had invested such a lot of time in me. I couldn't let the donor family of my new heart down either. The next morning I went back into the operating room. After a few days of further suffering, my bowels started to move. I felt more energetic, my food intake increased and things started to look up. I was able to appreciate the rising sun each morning and I began looking forward to the daily visits from family and friends.

Three weeks later, on March 14, and against the advice of Dr. Ross, I went home. I made all sorts of deals with the nurses and doctors to gain my release. Having been in the hospital for over three months, I thought it was about time for me to get out of there and get on with my life. But leaving the hospital just then, was not a wise move on my part. I had a feeling that the nurses knew I would be back. When

My son-in-law Kevin Hope taking me home.

Kevin, my son-in-law, picked me up, it was a cold and snowy day outside. After a short drive to his home, Kevin carried me in his arms into the house. I was scared out of my wits—if he dropped me, I could be in serious trouble and I'd be back in the hospital much faster than anticipated. But at my daughter's home in Toronto, I tried to show off a little too much as I walked unescorted from the kitchen to the living room. My legs gave out and I fell, hitting my head on the floor, which resulted in a small concussion and a large bruise on my head. My fever started to rise and a quick call to the hospital confirmed my greatest fear. I had to go back after less than twenty hours of freedom.

It was again a miserable day when Kevin drove me back to the hospital. My doctors knew that I was coming back. The nametag on my former bed was still attached. I had a bad case of pneumonia and excess fluid in my lungs. Needless to say, I was very depressed. A few days later, on March 19, I went back for the fourth time into the operating room. Drainage tubes were inserted into my right lung in order to remove further accumulated fluid. A day after that operation, on March 20, I felt ready to die again. I kept on saying that I was not feeling right and that something was bothering me. The next day I went into a coma and the doctors were at a loss as to what to do; little could be done at that point. All my vital signs were normal, except my kidneys. After an MRI test was done, I was put on kidney dialysis and received a number of blood transfusions. This was a very hard time for my wife and the whole family. For five days they saw a lifeless body in that bed that didn't move or say a word—it didn't complain or even ask for a Popsicle.

The many prayers by friends and family and the care of the attending physician, Dr. Ross and others, helped in my miraculous recovery. On the fifth day, with my wife by my side and the radio providing the only sound to break the perpetual silence that had been hanging over the room those past several days, I regained consciousness. I don't remember a thing from that time, but I am told that we broke out in tears and thanked the Lord.

This was a difficult time for my three children, particularly for my oldest son, Peter. He felt very uncomfortable seeing me in that condition. It made it very hard for him to have conversations with me. All we ever talked about was going on a fishing trip or playing golf together. Martin put up a much braver front; he would remind me about the good old days—the awards I had won, the things we had done together, the good times we had had at Disney World and other places. Jackie was harder to figure out. She always smiled, she was happy and cheerful and showed very few signs of depression. But Jackie is a great actor, and thank God all my children are positive thinkers. Despite the seriousness of the situation, we shared a lot of laughs, and I had a feeling of togetherness and closeness as a family. On April 9, my sister Lieselotte and my brother-in-law Karl who, on their way from wintering in Florida, stopped by the hospital. It was a tearful reunion. I'm not sure if they were prepared to see me in that condition. I remember waiting in a chair next to my bed, and after the nurses had made my bed, Karl picked me up and lifted me with one swoop onto my bed. Not bad for a seventy-one-year-old person. But by then my weight had fallen below one hundred pounds. After a two-hour visit they left, and in a way I was relieved. I couldn't stand too much sympathy.

I soon found a way to get occasional relief from that unappetizing hospital food. Rosemarie would take me underground in a wheelchair to The Hospital for Sick Children, where they had a great buffet-style cafeteria. We would sit by the window and watch the traffic go by, reminiscing about all the good times we had had and would have again. My outlook was always positive.

The following thirteenth of April was our thirty-fourth wedding anniversary. Rosemarie, in her efficient way, had planned a special dinner for the two of us. She had taken care of all the arrangements to celebrate this joyous feast, and since I was unable to walk, she arranged for a wheelchair to transport me to dinner in a private tenth-floor conference room. She decorated the table with a fine linen cloth and napkins. She brought our best china and silver from home. Fresh flowers, candles and a bottle of champagne with crystal glasses were placed on the table. Southern-fried chicken was the entrée, my favourite. After being on hospital food for three months, anything tasted good. Only someone who knows Rosemarie could understand her desire to please me, and it was a very special dinner that I will never forget. Just thinking about it brings tears to my eyes. After the dinner we went back to my room to greet my children, who joined in our celebration. It was a very warm and spiritual celebration. A burning desire overcame me, making me anxious to get started with my newly-given life.

By this time my stay in the hospital had already lasted four months. My daily routine mainly consisted of identifying and recognizing the sounds outside my room. I was able to recognize Rosemarie's footsteps as well as those of Dr. Ross as they were coming down the corridor and approaching my room. I was so delighted to see them each day. Rosemarie waited on me hand-and-foot and willingly fulfilled many pleasant as well as not so pleasant tasks. Dr. Ross always had positive news for me. I just loved her cheerful disposition. Thank God for doctors with these wonderful attributes.

Finally, on April 28, 1997, 128 days after I had been admitted into the hospital as a transplant patient, the day came when I could finally go home. Armed with tons of medication and a handful of medical books and data on what to do and what not to do, I was free at last. With a new heart in my chest and the old one left behind, we drove into God's country, my beloved Georgian Bay. It was possibly the most beautiful drive up Highway 400 that I have ever taken. Many thoughts were going through my head then. How was I going to live my new life? What was I going to do? Would the new heart be happy with this old body, or would I face a lot of rejections and other problems? Realizing that at age fifty-seven I had received a new lease on life, I was determined to make this new start to my life a good and productive one.

Since we lived alone, we had given little thought as to how I would get out of the car and into my home—at that point, I was still unable to walk or stand alone on my own two feet. The first hurdle to overcome was stepping over a simple ten-inch tall step at our entrance door. With just the two of us there, we were suddenly faced with the question of how I would get around, have a shower or climb the stairs to my bedroom. All the physiotherapy that I had to do in the hospital did not prepare me for this. But it did not take all that long to adjust; Rosemarie improvised a number of aids that were of great help in getting me around more efficiently. I had a support walker for my daily walks around the block. We had a raised toilet seat installed so I could stand up on my own after use. We rigged a step-in and step-out ramp for the bathtub. Every time I had a bath or shower, Rosemarie had to wrap me up in Saran Wrap to keep my drainage tubes clean and prevent infection. I felt like a piece of meat ready to go into the freezer.

The next two weeks went by quite well. I took my daily walk around the block with the assistance of the walker. I was trying very hard to get back into some sort of shape, as I could see my friends playing golf from my window and I was determined to join them very soon. But unfortunately, it was not quite the right time for that; I was to go back to the hospital for a third time. The joy of being in one's own home had lasted for all of two weeks; the drainage tubes were not draining the fluid from my lungs properly and I was accumulating more fluid. The odour from the tubes was hardly Chanel No. 5. As a matter of fact, it was much better to stay a fair distance away from me. If you could not see me, you sure could smell me. Back I went to the hospital.

On May 11, 1997 Dr. Todd, head of thoracic surgery at Toronto General, replaced the tubes with a claggett window, or an open window thoracostomy, which is an opening on the right side of the ribcage, about five by three inches. In most cases, and with proper care, the opening heals and will close by itself in a period of six to twelve months. In some cases, surgery might be needed to help the closing process.

I was convinced that, given enough time, it would close on its own soon enough. But unfortunately that did not happen. Other than not being able to go swimming, I have no other restrictions. My golf game is good, and because of my condition I receive a lot of sympathy and extra strokes from my golfing buddies. Five days after the operation for the claggett window, I was allowed to go home. The day was May 16, one day before my fifty-eighth birthday. It was quite a homecoming. My weight was down by about fifty-five pounds and I was still unable to walk or climb up stairs. I rested and slept in a pullout couch downstairs in my home and for the next while it became my bed. But after two nights, I wanted to sleep in my own bed. Rosemarie put a rope under my arms and pulled me up the stairs, step by step. Thinking back, it must have been a rather pathetic sight. I laugh about it today, but before my transplant, that climb up the stairs was a real ordeal for me. By the time I made it up the stairs at night, I was blue in the face, my fingernails had turned blue and it took some twenty minutes before my heart would settle down. But that's all history now. My dog Molly and I play a little game now where we race up the stairs to see who gets to the top first. A happy animal can be a real blessing to your health.

On May 19 I had my first biopsy after the heart transplant at the hospital. We left the house at 5:30 a.m. in order to be ready for the biopsy with Dr. Daly at 8:00 a.m. As we arrived at the front door of the hospital, my wife opened the car door to help me out. Being stubborn as always, I refused to use a wheelchair, but my trying to be a hero did not last long. Within seconds my legs gave out and they collapsed right under me. I fell flat on my back on the sidewalk. A number of kind people came running to assist Rosemarie, who was unable to get me up by herself, and someone ran to find a wheelchair. With only my pride and ego slightly damaged, I was able to continue my journey. A week later I had an appointment with my local family doctor, and as I was sitting in the waiting room, unbeknownst to me, a lady whose two children had the chickenpox walked in. I am sure it was then that I was infected, because three days later I had a full-blown case of the shingles. Due to the rejection drugs I was taking, my immune system was down and suppressed. Never really having known what shingles were, I learned very quickly that it was a very painful infection—one that was attacking the nerve endings on the left side of my body. So now I had the claggett window on the right side of my ribcage and the shingles had taken over the left side. The front part was just beginning to heal from the transplant. When my family doctor, Dr. Brian Marshall, saw the opening on one side and the shingles on the other, he just about fainted. Little did I know that these shingles were very stubborn and would plague me for the next eighteen months.

Now I am full of energy and can't wait to get out of bed at seven o'clock every morning. There is so much living to be done. It's a great feeling to wake up and see the sun rise through my bedroom window. For a long time, the joy and exhilaration of working up a real sweat on the treadmill, or being on the road in the warm summer months, or going cross-country skiing in the winter—these had eluded me. All that has changed now. My next goal is to resume my work; I feel my life will be complete again.

Throughout my twenty-five years of suffering from heart disease and spending many weeks and months in various hospitals facing numerous operations, I never lost faith. Faith, that is, in the Lord. My very positive attitude helped me through it. There is no way that I could have fought this battle on my own. Each and every operation I faced was approached with a very positive attitude and with the knowledge that it was going to be a success. The fear of not surviving the operation never entered my mind. I am sure that this conviction played a great role in my survival. You can get up in the morning and talk or think yourself into any condition: "Oh, it's raining, I am sure I will get a headache; there's thunder rolling in, I can feel my bones aching."

Get rid of these negative thoughts and think positive. There's nothing to be gained by not adopting a very healthy, positive mindset. All of the transplant patients I interviewed for this book had one thing in common: a very positive mind. The problem with most of us is that we will find an excuse for every situation and complain about the smallest detail. It becomes part of our daily routine. Be thankful for what you have and what you are blessed with. There is always someone who is much worse off than you are. Nobody wants to listen to a chronic complainer. I don't want to hang around or associate with a bunch of complaining, miserable people. The habit of being negative and unhappy for no real reason is contagious. We are very fortunate to live in a country blessed with abundant resources, wealth and human compassion; it is much more than we can say for some parts of the world. There are few countries as generous in donating money, food and care for others as Canada. Per capita, we are right on top, and perhaps someday we will reach the same summit with our organ donations. Remember, "the mind controls the body."

Today, for instance, when I awoke, I suddenly realized that this was the best day ever of my life. There were times when I wondered if I would ever make it to this day, but I did. And because I did, I'm going to celebrate. I'm going to celebrate the unbelievably rich and rewarding life I have had so far: the accomplishments, the many blessings and, yes, even the hardships, including all of my experiences as a heart transplant patient. All of this has made me a stronger and better person. Today, I celebrate all those good and helpful people that I had the pleasure of meeting in my life. In particular those who stayed with me through thick and thin.

Tonight, before I say my prayers when I go to bed, I'll go outside and raise my eyes to the heavens. I'll stand in awe of the beauty of the stars and the moon, and I will praise God for these magnificent treasures.

Postscript: On November 24, 1999 Dr. Todd of the Toronto General Hospital performed perhaps one of his last operations in Canada before leaving to practice in the U.S. The claggett window in my right side was finally closed. Despite being told that I would never swim again, three months later I was in the ocean in Florida. The waiting game was over, the operation was a success. I had hoped that it would be a while before I'd have to see a hospital from the inside again. But this was not to be. On August 1, 1999 we went for a two-week visit to our good friends Bev and Rainer in Maryland. It was late in the afternoon when we pulled up in the long driveway to their farm. This venture had a very bad start. As we stepped out of the car in Maryland, our friends' dog, a female Airedale, attacked our dog Molly, a female Irish Terry, a breed of the same family that are hostile to each other. I, of course, had to play referee, but paid dearly for it. The Airedale did not like my interference, and showed it by giving me two four-inch gashes in the upper calf of my right leg.

Since this was a horse farm, Rainer rushed into the barn, got a bottle of iodine and a supply of tensor bandages used for horses, and took care of my bleeding wound before the ambulance arrived. The leg was stitched up at the closest hospital, and after receiving a tetanus shot and an infusion of antibiotic, I was sent home that same evening. How lucky can I be, they didn't even keep me overnight, was my first thought. Two days went by and my leg started to look like a red inflated balloon. I immediately went to see Bev's friend Dr. Carolyn Harrington and without hesitation she ordered me back into the hospital. I had contracted a major infection, which had seemed to be from a normal dog bite. For five days I was put on large doses of antibiotics and, thank goodness, the leg started to heal. Despite the suggestion of plastic surgery, my leg healed very well in a reasonably short time and today looks perfectly normal.

In July 2000, Rosemarie and I took our Airstream trailer up to St. Joseph's Island in northern Ontario for a two-week holiday. Again I ended up in a one-person hospital at the island. I was in the process of hooking up my trailer to the pull vehicle when the hitch tensions bar snapped and hit my left lower leg, this time creating a gash that took eight stitches to close. The doctor felt that antibiotics were not necessary, but it was most important to keep the wound clean. The healing process took about four weeks, a little longer then expected.

The moral of the story is that despite having a depressed immune system, the body still has enough fighting power to take care of us transplant patients. One can only marvel at this wonderful creation. Do everything you can to take good care of it.

Reaping the Rewards of Giving

> If you want happiness for an hour—take a nap.
> If you want happiness for a day—go fishing.
> If you want happiness for a year—inherit a fortune.
> If you want happiness for a lifetime—help someone else.

It is important that we are aware of how the mind controls the body and how negativity destroys it. The Lord controls destiny, while doctors help control its direction. The power of prayer, the greatest asset that we have, gives us strength and hope. It is the catalyst of all well-being. The love and enjoyment of life, its beauty, and its trials and tribulations are the foundation of a well-planned future. Caring and expressing one's love for another, the enjoyment of sharing, giving and receiving, these are the building blocks to a rewarding life.

To reach inner peace and satisfaction in the art of living and giving is a goal that few attain. Although we may have the talent and means to share our good fortune with others, we often fall short of doing this in our day-to-day actions. In church on Sunday, dig deep in every pocket for a donation. This in itself can be an act that brings satisfaction. Giving brings much greater rewards than receiving. To get our priorities straight is one of life's great challenges. To find comfort and peace in the knowledge that one has helped others despite, or because of our affluent lifestyle, carries great rewards.

Hours before my transplant operation I made a deal with God. "Lord, please guide me and give me the strength to survive what lies ahead of me. Let me enjoy my wife, family and friends for many years to come. Preserve and protect my body from infectious diseases. In return, Lord, I promised to adopt one more child from your earth. I will care for one who is less fortunate than we are and who is desperately depending on us. Please, Lord, be on my side in these next hours of need, and in the following days, weeks and years."

Just weeks after my return from the hospital, Rosemarie and I adopted our second child through World Vision Canada, little Rogerio Dos Santos Anunciacao, a three-year-old boy from Brazil. When I told my story to a minister of the church, he told me that no one should ever make deals with the Lord, but I'm not sure if I agree with him. I happen to be a deal-making kind of guy, and I think the Lord knows that. The deal is that when one gives, one also receives; for one can always take joy in giving joy to others.

The Power of Prayer

Is it only Christians who speak to God in prayer? You know the answer. We may get the notion that only a few pray to God regularly, and the rest only when we are in real trouble. Almost everyone who is in deep trouble will call on God. "There are no atheists in foxholes," goes the saying. Mrs. Pratico, the mother of fifteen-month-old Sophia, who received a new heart, said, "This sure changed our thinking. I have prayed more now than ever in the last fourteen months. I believe He heard our prayers."

But why do we leave everything to the last minute? Why do we procrastinate? God understands that He can help us. Don't leave your relationship with the Almighty till it's too late or until you are in desperate need. Establish a good relationship now, don't wait. Thank Him; speak to Him each and every day. Make a place for Him in your daily life. A life without God is like a boat without a captain. Where will it end up?

Many people of celebrity speak of their prayer life. Vanna White says, "I think one of the greatest things I do to show my children love is praying with them every night before they go to bed." Basketball star Michael Jordan said he was retiring in part because he wanted to spend more time with his children, and publicly said, "I read the Bible a lot.…I see that whatever happens, happens for a reason. I wouldn't be here without the will of God.…I learned that God is in charge."

At the age of eleven, I made a simple cross. It was just two bamboo shoots tied together with a string of raffia. It hangs in my bedroom and has been with me and has blessed my home for the past forty-eight years. My old Bible, which I read every night no matter where I am, was given to me on my first confirmation at the tender age of thirteen. It has been a source of much inspiration and strength in my everyday life. I had tough times, times when it was very hard to put on a happy face and be nice to everyone. But these were quickly overcome with positive thoughts. I made a promise, no matter what I had to go through, I would not make other people around me miserable because of my ill health. It would not solve anything or help my situation. Unfortunately, I feel I wasn't always successful in keeping that promise.

Rosemarie and I did a lot of communicating with the Lord when I was in the hospital. I remember very well the hours before my transplant, which was the most critical time. I needed assurance that everything was going to turn out for the best. It did. It doesn't matter who you are or what religion you belong to, as long as you have a strong belief and pray to your God. Keep the line of communication open throughout your life and not just in times of personal need.

My philosophy is simple. The Lord has guided and helped my family and me with numerous problems. I don't ask Him to make me win the lottery or to improve the performance of my mutual funds. I pray for peace, health and inner strength. To look myself in the mirror each and every morning and see what I think is a decent person, despite my shortcomings, and to be seen as such by others around me, is more important than any material wealth. It is also important in times of need to have good friends who support you spiritually as well as physically. We were blessed with a number of great friends. For example, there was one neighbour, Rejean, who built a beautiful outdoor deck upon my arrival home from the hospital, and Marie Anne and Dr. Sarne, who spent hours and days by my bedside. And then there were Thane and Ollie MacNeill, who supplied me with Nova Scotia lobster sandwiches—nothing after that tasted quite as good. These fine people supported me and added a lot to my inner strength.

The power of prayer is the greatest ally you can have. I feel that I am blessed with four factors that have kept me alive and happy throughout the past twenty-five years. Without those I would have never made it. They are:

- first, the power of prayer;
- second, a very positive mind;
- third, a great family and wonderful doctors; and
- finally, a strong desire to live a full and happy life.

The following is one of my favourite prayers. I found it in an old book in the attic in my parents' home. The first time I read it was at the age of thirteen, when I had just joined the CVJM, a religious association for young men. It was there that I was first introduced to Jesus.

Believe me, what I went through would have been absolutely impossible without having God on my side. Rosemarie and I spend many hours praying together and do you know what? It gave us strength to get through it all. It made me appreciate the sun rising and the birds singing when I might have been trapped in the depths of despair. I could have never gone through this alone. Thank you, Lord, for being on my side.

A Daily Prayer

I was given health that I might do greater things;
I was given infirmity that I might do better things.
I asked God for strength that I might achieve;
I was made weak that I might learn to obey.
I asked for riches that I might be happy;
I was given poverty that I might be wise.
I asked for power and the praise of men;
I was given weakness to sense my need of God.
I asked for all things that I might enjoy life;
I was given life that I might enjoy all things.
I got nothing I asked for but everything I hoped for;
In spite of myself, my prayers were answered.
I am among all men most richly blest.
Yes, God always gives us what's best for us.

— Gard W. DeHaan

— two —

Keeping Healthy
After an Organ Transplant

Life After an Organ Transplant

What is life? How do we measure it? Is it just a time measured in years or months to be lived here on earth ... or is it forever? Who really knows? The one thing we all hope for is that we will be able to live a long and fulfilling life, that we will have as much time as possible to share with our loved ones.

An organ transplant gives a person a new lease on life. But the challenges don't end with the operation. James McLaren received a new heart some four years ago. He is an active spokesperson on organ transplantation and on the part of its governing bodies in British Columbia. "Nobody said transplantation was an easy way out and that it is a cure. It is not. It is merely exchanging an unmanageable end-stage organ disease for a situation that can be controlled. It is our responsibility to look after ourselves now and the occasional problems are not problems, they are challenges. Challenges that we can and will meet."

Every transplant patient's case should be judged on an individual basis. Some people have problems with medication, some face possible rejection of the new organ, others gain weight because of the high dose of Prednisone, a cortisone-like drug that helps prevent rejection. In Canada, we have a small number of transplant patients who have successfully received a second heart, and I am one of these fortunate ones. On October 24, 1998, Dr. Ross took me off Prednisone to help me get back to my original weight. But other than a little weight gain (I am now back to my original weight) and the reoccurrence of a number of skin lesions on my face, I suffer from very few other side effects. Hopefully, within the next few years, our medications will improve, and new and innovative drugs will make the entire procedure easier on our bodies. There is a lot of research being done in the field of organ transplantation and someday doctors will treat a transplant in the same way that bypass surgery is performed today, as mere routine.

Rejection of the donated organ by the recipient's immune system is a major potential problem, and a cardiac biopsy is the only reliable way, at the present time, of diagnosing rejection. The procedure is done under local anesthetic. A bioptome, a small wire lead, is inserted through a small incision in the interior jugular vein on the right side of your neck or the upper chest area, and a number of small pieces of tissue are taken from the new heart you have received and examined for rejection. This process is performed at regular intervals for the rest of a transplant patient's life. However, Jim Gleason, a heart recipient in Pennsylvania, reports that the Hospital of the University of Pennsylvania (HUP) has changed that practice. If a patient has been rejection-free for five years after the transplant and is otherwise in good health, the invasive neck or chest biopsy is no longer performed. "All of this is new for us at HUP," says Jim. However, patients still attend a clinic every six months and take the traditional anti-rejection drugs.

The whole procedure of a biopsy takes about fifteen to twenty minutes. It is very reassuring to the transplant patients to know that there is a tremendous group of doctors and nurses backing us up, to look after us till death do us part. We are, without a doubt, the most cared after human beings on this earth.

Regular biopsies every three to six months and the occasional angiogram are still mandatory here in Canada. The other safety factor is attending a clinic each month or after each biopsy where a blood test is done, your weight is taken, medication is reviewed, changed or adjusted, and any problems, even those of a personal nature, are discussed.

Current Frequency of Biopsies after Transplantation:

First four weeks:	weekly
Weeks five to twelve:	every second week
Months four to six:	monthly
Months seven to twelve:	every second month
After one year:	every three to six months.

Dr. Paul Daly,
Division of Cardiology,
Toronto General Hospital

I spoke with Dr. Paul Daly, MD, FRCP, Division of Cardiology, Director of the CICUI of cardiology at Toronto General Hospital, on biopsies and post-transplant life.

Q: *Will we ever find a less invasive way than the biopsy to check for rejection?*

A: We have tried many creative ways in finding an alternative or less invasive way of checking for rejection, but at present the biopsy is still the best way. It gives us the most accurate results.

  The irony is that first we give the patient a new heart and then we take it back, piece by piece. Biopsy is a safe but rather inconvenient procedure, but it is very effective.

Q: *Can a patient feel or sense rejection?*

A: No, if you are sick with rejection, it is way too late. If we find only two cells out of 10,000, you are not sick, there is nothing you will notice or feel. Now, if you have 1,000 cells out of 10,000 that are easily defined by an echogram or blood marker or, of course, the biopsy, you are sick. If we were to wait till the patient is sick, then it is way too late. Early detection is very important.

Q: *Any advice for transplant patients, Dr. Daly?*

A: Stay healthy, don't be a sick person. Post-transplant life is tough; there are a number of things that need to be looked after. Things like don't neglect your medication, issues related to post-op follow-up on side effects from the medication. All of that needs to be properly looked after.

Beyond the physical challenges that face the organ recipient lies the psychological challenge of putting the operation sufficiently in the background and learning not to dwell on it. Get on with your life, do what you would like to do. Just don't ignore your health. Listen to your body; when you need a rest, take a rest. Find the right balance between an active but also relaxed lifestyle.

—•—

The medical staff is very sensitive to the personal as well as to the medical well-being of the patient. One is never alone; it is a joy to go to a clinic and meet transplant people who will become close friends, someone to share information and stories and, perhaps, to lean on in tougher times.

The Freedom to Choose

Thank God we live in a free country that allows us to make personal choices as to how to live our lives. We have freedom of religion, freedom of speech and freedom to choose any doctor who we feel will be best suited to looking after our personal well-being.

It is vitally important that you are comfortable and happy with the doctor you have chosen. Not every doctor is the same, not every doctor has the same training or mentality or is up-to-date with the very latest in medical advancements. Get opinions from other patients. Look for statistics and valuable information. Explore every possibility. The Internet is an endless source of information. It's your life and you're in charge of it. Manage it well.

After my first heart attack in 1974, I was under the care of a cardiologist for post-care treatment. A few weeks later I was released from the hospital and was feeling quite good. I changed my eating habits and exercised regularly, keeping track of my heart rate both before and after exercise. I made notes of all my daily activities. Armed with all of this information, I went to see this doctor for my follow-up appointment three months after the attack. He glanced quickly over my notes and dismissed them, saying, "It doesn't mean anything." He made it quite clear that my months or years were numbered. That was twenty-five years ago. Needless to say, I did not return to that doctor. He was negative, ill-informed and gave me little hope or incentive to ever see him again.

It is very important that you select a knowledgeable doctor, one who is right for you. Canada is blessed with many qualified medical practitioners in every area of specialization; make sure the one you choose fits that bill. Don't be afraid to get second and third opinions. It's your life; take charge and don't leave it in the hands of someone else.

The Power of a Positive Mind

Infection

Smiling is infectious,
You catch it like the flu.
When someone smiled at me today
I started smiling too.

I walked around the corner
And someone saw my grin.
When he smiled, I realized
I had passed it on to him.

I thought about the smile
And realized it's worth.
A single smile like mine, or yours
Could travel around the earth.

If you feel a smile begin,
Don't leave it undetected.
Let's start an epidemic quick
And get the whole darned world INFECTED.

— Author unknown

Much has been written about the effects of positive thinking and the old saying, "The mind controls the body." Heart disease struck me down at the age of thirty-four. It seemed to become a never-ending fight. But looking back now, I realize that somehow I did enjoy many pleasant and fun-filled times. My mind did not defeat me. I am an absolute believer in the importance of having a positive attitude. I see proof of this day after day, whether I am taking on a new project or playing on the golf course. Positive thoughts can bring success to everyone who takes the times to evaluate them.

But to have a very positive mind while ignoring what the body tells you and hoping the symptoms will go away, or laughing it off with the comment, "Nothing ever happens to me," is not a very smart way to manage your life. Thinking positively about the condition of your health (not just wishing it away) and doing something about it is smart thinking. Doing nothing, and hoping and waiting that it will go away is playing a dangerous game with your life.

Throughout my twenty-five-year ordeal with heart disease, it never entered my mind that my life could end because of it. I always saw the light at the end of the tunnel. I knew and prayed that the sun would shine again. After every rainstorm and cloudy day, the sun shines again. With the operations I have faced in the past twenty-five years, including my heart transplant, very seldom did my mind wander into negative or grey territory and stay there.

Reader's Digest, in its June 1999 issue, featured an article on Fred Bruemmer, a professional photographer who has the uncanny ability to get close to wild animals and is one of the top wildlife photographers in the world. Fred received a new heart in 1986, and today he is as active as ever. He just recently returned from exploring the forests in Bialowieza National Park in Poland. "He is one of the oldest heart transplant survivors in Canada," says his son Ayrel, a doctor. "But that's because Dad has this immense drive to keep coming back, to rediscover himself."

No matter how tough it gets, a positive attitude is perhaps the strongest ally one can have. Think of your wife, your kids and friends, think of your donor. Do you want to let all those people down? Whenever a negative thought crosses your mind, dismiss it and think of something pleasant—the fun time you had with your kids, your last vacation, or perhaps a newborn grandchild. Think of the future; once you get past that big hurdle in front of you, it's a level playing field. The sun will shine again. Be positive; see the good side of every scenario. After every harsh winter, spring and summer surely follows. The circle of life follows the same pattern each and every season. There are times when things are not going as well as we would like them to, but think of all the good times you've experienced and all the wonderful times that can still lie ahead. With a positive mind you can control the health of your body. You can go through a day with a headache because the weather has changed, you can feel an aching in your bones because it is raining outside; you can feel a migraine coming on because you ate a certain food. The list is endless. Get up every morning and praise the Lord, be full of joy because you are fortunate enough to face another day. Make the best of that day and never again feel sorry for yourself. Don't become a burden to others and don't feel satisfaction in making others share the knowledge of your daily aches and pains. Get on with life, there is always someone out there much worse off than you.

—•—

I had parents who saw only the gloomy side of every scenario. My mother never found any joy in seeing the sun coming up or watching how after every rainstorm new life begins and the sun shines again. She thought only in a very negative way. I feel sorry for people who can't see the beauty in the smallest and perhaps simplest things that come their way: the blooming of a flower, the first snowfall, a child's smiling face, or just a walk in the park. There is so much we have that we can be thankful for. Every night when I watch the news on TV and see the plight that has befallen the people of the Balkan and Middle East nations or others in ravaged African countries, all I can say is, "Aren't we lucky."

Helen Keller was once asked what she thought was the worst calamity that could befall a person, and she replied, "To have eyes, yet fail to see." Too often we see only what we want to see without realizing what is really there.

Some years ago, Roger Whittaker recorded a great song, "The Wind Beneath My Wings." It says a lot about the way we feel and about the companion or the person who is always by our side. If you ever feel down, this song will truly give you a spiritual lift and give you new hope. One is often forgetful of the fact that a lot of people, especially loved ones, depend on you and think very lovingly of you. You are a pillar of strength to many people, don't let them down. Make people around you feel good, enjoy life and enjoy each day to the fullest. No one wants to listen to or hang around a loser, someone who complains about everything all the time. No one wants to listen to your problems, we all have our own. Be a ray of sunshine to others, a Mother Teresa with a passion for life. People love a winner, a positive person. He or she is much more fun to be with than the chronic complainer whom everyone tries to avoid.

Perhaps one of the greatest mind games is the game of golf. After the first shot that ends up in the water, already you may start thinking, "I think I'm going to have a lousy game today." Or when you're facing an intimidating water hazard, you may find yourself thinking, "I'll use an old ball here because it'll end up in the water anyway." How wrong can you be? Realize how a positive thought can improve your game. Think positive and say, "I'm going to hit a very sweet shot and drop it right next to the flag." It won't always work, but don't program your mind by thinking negative thoughts; think positive, take the newest ball you have in your bag and let it rip. In many aspects of life a positive mind is one the greatest gifts that one can possess. Your best education to think and act positive is to read a number of biographies on people like Henry Ford, the Rockefellers, Winston Churchill— these are high-powered giants of our century, but they all had one thing in common, a very positive mind.

Every crossroad you face, all the aches and pains you may experience may be small compared to the next person's. Don't let such things defeat you. The mind has a tremendous effect on your daily life. The mind controls your body; it can do wonderful things for you, but it can also destroy you.

My surgery was not going to be easy and I knew that from the outset, just as Sir Edmund Hillary knew when he climbed Mount Everest that "You can't do it in a four-wheel-drive or an ATV. To reach the summit, you must claw yourself up, inch by inch." Little did I know that some years later after my surgery, I would meet Sir Edmund in person at a photo session.

Remember the joke about the young boy who walked into a room filled to the ceiling with horse manure and said, "There has to be a pony in here somewhere." Now that is positive thinking.

These are some of my favourite books on the power and control of our mind:

- *Enter the Zone*, by Barry Sears, Ph.D., Regan Books, 1995.
- *Positive Living and Health*, by Mark Bricklin, Mark Golin, Deborah Grandinetti and Alex Lieberman, Rodale Press, 1990.
- *Love, Medicine & Miracles*, by Bernie S. Siegel, MD, Harper and Row, 1988.
- *Head First—The Biology of Hope*, by Norman Cousins, E.P. Dutton, 1989.

—•—

"A positive attitude won't let you do anything,
But it will let you do everything better than
A negative attitude will."

Keeping Fit

After the initial recovery period, it feels a little like New Year's Eve. All sorts of resolutions and changes for the next while are implemented. Things like regular exercise, a change of diet, no smoking or drinking, and less stress and worry are on the agenda. That is great, but remember to stick with it. The success is not in holding to your resolutions and promises just in the first few months, but in continuing with them for the rest of your life. Your body is like a finely tuned machine or a well-trained athlete, it needs to burn up energy. I remember Dr. Daly saying, "Listen to your body." If you ever feel down or weak, or if you've had a late night, it is better to sit out a day rather than push too hard.

The exercise program that works for me might not satisfy your needs. I exercise every day. I spend forty minutes each day doing fast walking, which is just as good as jogging. After that I spend about fifteen minutes lifting ten-kilo weights and doing some stretching on the floor. I also cross-country ski in the winter and play golf in the summer. Of course, my dog Molly needs to be taken on walks, and I love riding my bike. Canoeing and hiking are forms of exercise I enjoy as well.

I often think back to all the times prior to my heart transplant when I was watching TV or just looking out my window over the golf course, watching people having fun and enjoying life. I was jealous, and my dreams were that someday I would do all those things again.

One needs to stay healthy and fit. Exercise, such as fast walking for about five kilometres every day or every second day, plus biking for forty-five minutes four times a week, is a good exercise regimen to maintain. Supplement this with hiking, cross-country skiing or canoeing, or perhaps by playing golf.

The greatest waste of time is to sit in front of the TV day in, day out. Very little is accomplished. Inactivity, such as being a couch potato carries greater risk of heart disease than smoking. Get up, get out and start to enjoy your newfound life. You received a gift, a gift from a very generous donor; with that comes the responsibility to take good care of it. Keep your mind active.

We have a number of choices we can make to keep healthy. First of all, don't smoke. Every cigarette that one smokes shortens the life span by five minutes. It may be hard to give up, but if you cherish your life, stopping is an absolute must. Eat nutritious food, including plenty of fresh vegetables, fruits and nuts, fish and lean meats. Exercise regularly, lead a happy and stress-free life, have a loving, supporting family and find a good doctor who understands you and your medical history.

Eating Healthy

With a new lease on life comes the responsibility of taking good care of that very precious gift we have been given. As a transplant recipient, our responsibility to the donor family must be taken seriously, even if it requires a drastic life change. Besides actively engaging in a regular exercise program, one needs to control the type and the quantity of food intake.

Before 1920, few countries reported or recorded many cases of heart disease. In Japan and China, as well as in Germany, heart disease was virtually unknown. England, prior to World War II, led the nations with the highest incidence of heart disease. Why have things changed so dramatically in the past fifty years? I am convinced that much has to do with our food intake, the type of food that is mass marketed and factory produced. Our daily diet has changed; we no longer eat healthy, home-grown vegetables and home-cooked meals. Too often, we fill ourselves with prepared, frozen, fatty and fast foods that are loaded with cholesterol and carbohydrates. Very few of these important nutritious ingredients that the body needs in order to stay healthy are present in our modern-age fast food.

Prior to and many years after World War II, many people in Germany, as well as in Britain, Japan and many other parts of the world, had vegetable gardens and ate plenty of fresh fruits, vegetables and fish. Meat was rather scarce and expensive, so they ate whatever was available. That kind of diet was good for them. Then the modern era began. Fast food joints sprang up everywhere, frozen and factory-prepared foods took over healthy, homegrown and pesticide-free staples. Chemical sprays and pesticides were the standard byproducts of the fruits and vegetables industry. Only recently have we learned that heart disease and cancer, despite many medical advances and new ways of combating these, are on the rise, and that the over-consumption of processed or hydrogenated fast foods are suspected to be a significant factor. Often both parents are working and little time is devoted to preparing a healthy home-cooked meal. A plot in the backyard that in former days might have been occupied by a vegetable garden now often serves as a new location for a swimming pool, and our fruit orchards are being quickly replaced by subdivisions.

Meanwhile, we have adopted a very fast pace in our lifestyle, the ever-important dollar dictates our daily activity and little time is set aside for relaxing. We have done very little to prepare ourselves for this very demanding lifestyle. The ever-present TV has done little to motivate or inspire us to get out and exercise.

Soon enough, the human heart will say, "Enough of this. I can't keep up with all this stress, and get by on such bad fuel and so little exercise. Help!" This, explained in my own very simple way, contributed to the start of heart disease, which claims thousands of lives every year. In the U.S. and in Canada, a heart attack occurs every twenty seconds.

Our fuel is the food we consume, it helps us function and provides us with the necessary energy to maintain a healthy, useful, active lifestyle. Due to my family's long history of heart disease, members of my family have always been careful eaters. I left the hospital in May 1997 weighing less than a hundred pounds, but two years later my weight had ballooned to 172 pounds, which was too much for my five-foot-four frame. I then started my Dr. Atkins diet, a very low-carbohydrate meal plan that never lets you starve but allows you to lose weight quite quickly. Once or twice a week we have a fish meal, followed by a vegetarian or a meatless dish. The rest of the week I could have all the eggs and bacon I liked. But I don't think this is a healthy diet for the long term. Check with your doctor first before starting on such a regimen. The dietary suggestions that Rosemarie and I follow are from the book by Andrew Weil, MD, *Eating Well For Optimum Health*, published by Alfred A. Knopf. What Dr. Weil says makes a lot of sense and the guidelines can be easily followed. I recommend the book very highly.

My family eats a lot of fresh vegetables, particularly the cancer-fighting curative vegetables such as broccoli and cabbage, mostly grown in our backyard garden without the use of pesticides or fertilizer. It always amazes me how simple and productive it is to maintain a sixteen-by-eight-foot plot of garden. We have followed the old European tradition of eating most of our main meals at lunchtime. It is better for the digestive system, and sitting down after a big meal at night watching TV is a sure way of putting on those extra pounds and is not very healthy for you. I remember how as a child growing up in Germany, it was my job to bring a hot meal by bicycle to my father's workplace at noontime. In later days, when I was an apprentice at the workplace, we had our main meal at lunch as well. We had a large trough of hot water and by 11:30 a.m., all the metal canteens were submerged in hot water for thirty minutes to guarantee a hot meal.

There are a number of foods that one should eat rather sparingly. Foods such as hot dogs and hamburgers, and fried foods such as french fries are high in fat and cholesterol and low in nutrition. Time and again, it has been proven that these foods, consumed on a frequent basis, are not healthy for anyone.

In February 1999, the U.S. Health and Food Administration released a new study about the connection between cancer and junk food. Just look around you: 85 percent of North Americans are overweight, and this is largely due to the foods we eat. I love a grilled hamburger with a cool beer as much as the next guy. Except I make mine with extra-lean beef, avoiding any chemical additives such as meat colouring and preservatives. Salt substitutes and natural herbs and spices are good alternatives as seasonings. Our body needs approximately one gram, about half a teaspoon, of salt per day. Everything else just becomes a burden on your heart. High quantities of salt in or on your food lead to fluid retention and high blood pressure that in turn can lead to heart problems, strokes and kidney failure. With extra fluid in your body, you gain weight and your heart has to work that much harder. We receive enough salt through the intake of store-bought goods such as bread, margarine, cereals, cold cuts, and cheeses, to give just a few examples. Just look at the salt or sodium levels listed on the ingredient labels of your purchased grocery items. Too much sugar in your daily diet is very much responsible for a lot of our weight gain. Sugar turns into fat. A low-carbohydrate diet in conjunction with regular exercise is a sure way to lose weight. Be aware of what you feed your body. Treat it like a shrine, it needs to last a long time.

Fresh fruits and vegetables are good for you; however, there is one fruit that a transplant patient on cyclosporine must avoid. My favourite breakfast fruit is grapefruit, and to me no breakfast is complete without it. But grapefruit, or its juice, can increase the cyclosporine level in your blood. If you feel you can't live without grapefruit juice for breakfast, make sure you check with your doctor first. Your blood level should be monitored. Your best bet would be to avoid it and switch to oranges or orange juice.

I now bake my own bread and breakfast buns and make my own pasta. This way, I control the ingredients as well as the salt content. Freshly baked bread has a great aroma and it tastes very delicious. In fact, our dog Molly likes it, too. One time I placed a freshly baked loaf of bread on the kitchen counter at night and went to bed. I had been looking forward to having some of the freshly baked bread for breakfast, but couldn't find it the next morning. After a little investigating and some gentle terrorization of Molly, I realized that she had had a good night with my bread. Needless to say, she did not eat breakfast that morning. But from then on, the bread always went directly into the refrigerator.

A good reference book for any kitchen on the harmful effects of food additives, and which foods are most beneficial to you, is *The Wellness Encyclopedia of Food and Nutrition* by Dr. Sheldon Margen. Dr. Margen is also the editor of "The Wellness Letter" published by the University of California at Berkeley.

There is much wisdom in the saying, "Breakfast like a king, lunch like a knave and dine like a pauper."

The Water We Drink

The water we drink and use for cooking is directly related to our health and well-being. People are paranoid about the quality of the water from our polluted lakes and streams. The industrial revolution and its irresponsible management have succeeded in destroying this most precious commodity.

After the tragic incident of E.coli (Escherichia coli) contamination in the water supply in Walkerton, Ontario, in June of 2000 that led to the death of six young people, the whole North American continent was made aware of the invisible danger to our health that can come from drinking a glass of contaminated water. Contaminated water has been with us for many years but we have found a number of different purification methods to make it acceptable for human consumption. The safest and most effective way to treat water is by distillation, heating the water to a high temperature and using the vapours that stay behind as your source of healthy and safe drinkable water. My wife and I have used an Echo-Water distiller for the past five years and are convinced of the benefits it brings. The distiller is distributed by Echo-Water in Toronto and sold through a number of outlets such as Sears. The cost is about a hundred and ninety dollars—it will produce three gallons of distilled water per day, more than you will actually need. That quantity suffices for all our drinking, cooking and coffee water. Each time we go to Florida, our distiller comes along with us. For making wine we use the same water. If you are interested in learning more about your drinking water, you can read an interesting book written by Dr. Allen E. Banik called *The Choice Is Clear*, published by Acres USA in 1989. It deals with the benefits of distilled water in the fight against arthritis, hardening of the arteries, glaucoma and diabetes, as well as with the health hazards that we are exposed to when drinking city tap water. It is a small investment with big returns. Transplant patients have a lower-than-normal immune system, and distilled water offers one more way of protecting one's health.

Filtered water is not always what it claims to be because of improper maintenance and the collection of harmful bacteria and chemicals in the filter itself. Bacteria thrive in the carbon filters, which is why Brita uses a disposable, activated silverized carbon filter. Doctors, fitness instructors and diet gurus advocate the drinking of eight glasses of water per day. Drinking lots of water is a healthy habit to adopt. But make sure that it is water that you can trust. Distilled water is a little like cooked food—all harmful bacteria are killed in the process. If the lack of fluoride in distilled water is a concern, remember that the proper additives in one's toothpaste can make up for it.

Restaurants now serve "designer" waters at enormous markups. Bottled water is a prerequisite for the workout set and gossip is exchanged around the ubiquitous water cooler in the office. In North America, people spend some 600 million dollars having their water filtered or treated in some way. Bottled water is big business. In 1997 Canadians drank about 292 million dollars' worth of bottled water. If the average person drinks about two litres of water a day, the cost of bottled water over a forty-year period would amount to $13,724 at current market value.

There is a dramatic differential between the cost of a one-time investment of a distiller at about $190 or a Brita filter at $30. Water is the lifeline to our well-being; make sure you carefully choose the kind of water you drink.

Alcohol Consumption

The HeartLinks newsletter features a number of articles on the benefits of drinking wine. One of the best red wines is Cabernet Sauvignon, which is a particularly good wine for promoting a healthy heart. Dr. Jean-Paul Broustet of Haut Léveque Hospital in Pessac, just south of the city of Bordeaux, has said that Cabernet Sauvignon grapes have high levels of resveratrol, a potent ingredient that increases the level of good cholesterol in one's blood and limits the production of artery-blocking bad cholesterol. "The highest concentrations of resveratrol are found in red wines, particularly in Cabernet Sauvignon," reported "The Heart," a British medical journal. Red grapes produce resveratrol to protect themselves from a potentially deadly fungus. They are also high in other antioxidants called polyphenols, which prevent cell damage from oxygen-containing chemicals called free radicals. Quercetin, another compound found in red wine, helps to dilate blood vessels and prevent blood clots.

Two other wines particularly good for promoting a healthy heart are Cellars Classic Rosso Grande and Magnotta's Merlot. The latter, a mellow, great-tasting wine, costs you about three dollars per bottle and is sold in a twenty-litre container as a finished wine for approximately eighty dollars. But with the increase in popularity of domestic as well as imported wines, the price of wine has risen and I have joined the many Canadians who make their own. You can produce an excellent product if you use pure grape juice or juice concentrate in the right way. After six weeks to six months, depending on what process you choose, you can bottle twenty-four to thirty 750-ml bottles of quality wine. In the past, much has been reported about contaminated wines—wines that have been exported to us mainly from Europe— that have contained antifreeze, milk, sodium, sugar and other additives. These are health hazards that are hard to detect. To avoid these problems, make your own wine and control the quality of the ingredients. Hard liquor is often too expensive in Canada unless you buy the occasional bottle duty free on a trip to the U.S.

Much research and printed material has been published on the benefits of wine consumption—in moderation, of course. Alcohol intake should be limited to one or two glasses of red or white wine per day, or one drink of hard liquor, according to the latest research. But many Canadians have misinterpreted this guideline. The potential health benefits associated with drinking wine don't serve as an excuse for consuming alcohol in large quantities. Moderation is the golden rule in alcohol consumption—as it is with many other things in life.

The Inner Clean Diet

Twice each year, usually after Christmas and in mid-June, my wife and I go on a six-day diet to remove the toxins from our body. Our body has millions of cells which, over time, get clogged up with acid, sugar, mucus and pus. When you feel you have very little pep, your appetite is poor, you don't sleep well, your complexion is bad and you suffer from aches and pains, it might be time for a little revitalization. A cleansing diet is as old as our civilization, and it can remedy that situation.

For six short days you will be on a feast—not a fast. You will be filling your body with nature's life-giving foods and fruits and vegetables, which contain all those precious vitamins and minerals. It is supplemented with cottage cheese, bread and coffee or tea. You truly do not suffer or go hungry on this diet. You just change your eating habits for six days. You will feel great and will lose about six to seven pounds in that week. Try it, we have recommended it to many people and know it works. The diet was designed by a Dr. Thurman Fleet in 1947 and has been used by thousands of people. (Readers interested in obtaining a copy of the original booklet by Dr. Fleet, which is no longer in print, can contact the author directly.

The body is somewhat like a car. If the fuel injection is clogged up, it needs cleaning. Mother Nature is your mechanic.

Nutritional Supplements: Are They Necessary?

The vitamins market is rapidly moving from its old "home remedy" roots to a high-tech future, generating millions of dollars in sales every year. Not all advertised vitamin and mineral supplements, however, are equal. One can spend a lot of money on supplements and end up with nothing more than expensive urine.

Nutritional supplements, such as vitamins A, C, E and garlic or calcium, are very valuable to your well-being. Calcium, for instance, is a very important supplement for the transplant patient because high doses of immunosuppressive drugs take a toll on your bones. Calcium has the power to strengthen the bone structure. Most foods, particularly fresh fruits and vegetables, as well as fish and red meats, offer your body a good, nutritious source of much-needed vitamins and minerals. Taking supplements is a very personal choice, but it is best to talk to your doctor or dietician before doing so, as some substances or "alternative therapies" can interfere with your medication.

I take 10,000 IU of vitamin A, 1,000 mg of vitamin C, 1,000 IU of vitamin E and three 500-mg doses of calcium per day, simply as a preventative. Little harm can be done, and very much can be gained by taking these supplements.

Vitamin A	The "miracle" vitamin, protects against cancer-causing agents.
Vitamin C	Also know as ascorbic acid, helps fight cancer.
Vitamin E	An important antioxidant, prevents heart disease and boosts the immune system.
Calcium	Our mothers have been telling us from time immemorial to drink our milk. It prevents and treats osteoporosis, is useful in preventing high blood pressure, lowers cholesterol and is helpful in preventing arthritis.
Garlic	Protects against heart disease, cancer and infection. Much has been said and written about the healing power of garlic, which is called "the Russian penicillin."

Aspirin	Just one of some twenty-four drugs known collectively as non-steroidal anti-inflammatory drugs. It is widely used and recommended by doctors to heart patients. Ask your doctor about the beneficial effects of aspirin.
Green Tea	There's nothing like "a cuppa tea" to soothe frazzled nerves. Now thanks to the latest research, we know tea is more than just a pick-me-up. Both black and eastern-style green tea have been shown to enhance the absorption of vitamin C, strengthen capillaries and inhibit the growth of malignant cancer cells. Recently, researchers in Japan showed that tea extracts could kill harmful intestinal bacteria, such as some strains of staphylococcus and salmonella.

It is not the long sought-after fountain of youth, but it might add years to your life or better yet, it may help to add life to your years. Green tea has long been renowned as a herbal healer. Modern scientific research has now confirmed that it offers real benefits for cancer, heart disease, immunity, longevity, mental acuity, diabetes, ulcers, weight control and osteoporosis. Ever since my operation, I have been searching for a substitute to increase my now-weakened immune system. Having done a lot of reading on the subject, I have come to the conclusion that drinking green tea from China is a good way to boost the immune system. A number of articles, particularly in the European magazines, have dealt with this topic. Two cups a day are sufficient. Does it work? Who knows, only time will tell. While both black and green tea are rich in antioxidants, green tea is also high in catechins, a natural heart protector. A cup of green tea may be good protection against skin cancer, possibly as good as sunscreen, as reported by some Australian researchers. A recently published booklet on the subject is sold in most health food stores or pharmacies and is called "All About Green Tea" by Victoria Dolby. It sells for $2.95 and is loaded with great information. A reference book listed in this excellent book is *The Doctor's Vitamin and Mineral Encyclopedia* by Dr. Sheldon Saul Hendler, published by Simon and Shuster, New York.

Taking vitamins or not is an individual's choice. But there is just too much well-researched evidence to dismiss the benefits of taking supplements of, for instance, vitamins C and E. Whatever you do, ask your doctor first. Each transplant patient takes different types and quantities of medication, but one fact that is common to all of us is that our medication needs to be taken each and every day, and always at the same time every day. That was at first a bit of a problem for me, but thanks to my wife, I have skipped my medication very few times, if any. I always carry an extra set of medication in my car as well as in Rosemarie's purse. No matter what we do or where we go, we always have a spare set.

Can Viagra Put a Little Zest in Your Life?

In a recent question posted on the Internet to Dr. Jeff Punch at the division of transplantation at the University of Michigan, a transplant patient expressed his concern about the use of the drug Viagra, the latest help for those with sexual erection problems. His reply was as follows: "There is no reported experience with Viagra in transplant patients on immuno-suppression. However, Viagra is known to be a potent modulator of cytochrome p-450 metabolism. What it means is that ingestion of the drug almost certainly alters the blood levels of cyclosporine and tacrolimus. Many other drugs do the same thing, including dilantin, coumadin, erythromycin, fluconazol and others. I believe that the safest practice would therefore be to monitor blood levels of cyclosporine or tacrolimus in patients taking these drugs when starting this medication."

James McLaren, vice-president of the Canadian Transplant Games Association, has some very sensible advice. "Do whatever you like with transplant advice and data from the Internet, but always check with your doctor or clinic first." There is a tremendous amount of information in print as well as on TV and on the Internet and it can be rather confusing at times. I believe most people who die or get into some very serious trouble with the use of Viagra in the act of intercourse are heart patients rather than transplant patients. There is a difference.

I believe that the situation of a person who has received a new heart through a transplant and wants to make use of Viagra is totally different from that of a person with a known heart condition, and I would not recommend in the latter case that one experiment with Viagra. Speaking from personal experience, I don't think that Viagra will necessarily help everyone who takes it. Personally, the results were not what were anticipated. The number of times it failed outnumbered the number of times it did not. The transplant patient is quite safe in giving it a try, but please check with your doctor first. It can be a rather expensive experiment.

I have spoken to Dr. Ross, who looks after some one hundred and fifty transplant patients at Toronto General Hospital. She sees very little reason not to use Viagra. "It can certainly improve the quality of you and your spouse's life."

We have only seen the tip of the iceberg; many more drugs like Viagra will be introduced to the market shortly. It will also bring the price per pill down to an affordable level. Just recently the media reported a "Viagra-like" drug which is made in Canada and is now available at price much lower than the current cost of Viagra, which sells for approximately fifty-five dollars for four pills.

Tips for the Travelling Transplant Patient

When travelling, careful planning is needed, whether it is a business trip to Winnipeg, a safari in East Africa or a stay in a first-class resort in the Caribbean, since your health can certainly affect your enjoyment of the trip. Dr. Ross had the following to say about travelling for transplant patients. "The only issue with travelling is we recommend that no out-of-country travel take place until at least six months after the transplant operation. Then, one is out of that risk period. Notify us prior to your travel, the coordinator will give you a travel letter that will help you in regards to carrying the drugs when confronted by customs. We have had patients travel to some pretty far-out and exotic places; we'd just like to know in advance so that we can be sure that immunization, vaccination and all medications are taken care of. I think it is great to see our transplant people travel throughout the world."

The hospital's travel information letter lists, among other things, all the important phone numbers you might need in case of an emergency. It lists current medications and required doses, any allergies you might have, your name and your ID number at the hospital. Make sure that you carry this document whenever you travel.

Take along a few extra days' supply of medication in case your departure is delayed. I can only speak from experience; on my last trip to Europe, our plane was twelve hours late and it was a good feeling to know that standby medication was available.

Time zone changes can make taking your medications right on time somewhat difficult. With as much as six to eight hours of time difference to some travel destinations, it is best to adjust the medication to the new local time and readjust on your return home. If you take your last dose of Cellcept MMF at ten o'clock at night in Canada, which would be four o'clock in Europe, when you get to Europe, continue taking the last medication at ten o'clock at night, local time. But please check with your doctor first to make sure that this arrangement is suitable for you.

If your destination is in a location with lots of sun, don't forget your sunscreen. As a transplant patient you are at great risk of developing skin cancer due to your immunosuppressive medication. I asked dermatologist Dr. Katarina Fiala why transplant patients tend to get a greater number of skin cancer lesions, and she confirmed that the transplant patient's immunosuppressive medication has much to do with it. "Everybody is susceptible to getting precancerous lesions and skin cancers in sun-damaged areas. However, they would likely develop and grow faster when you are on immunosuppression." Please protect yourself. Select a broad-spectrum sunscreen that blocks out the sun's shorter (UVB) rays and some of the longer (UVA) rays; check the labels for products containing oxybenzones, dibensoyl methane or benzophenones.

Dr. Fiala believes "the proper care is surgical removal. As far as precautions, other than using a strong sunscreen and avoiding the sun as much as possible, there is not much you can do. You should pay attention to any new lesions and get them removed as soon as possible."

Dr. Ivor Dreosti and his colleagues at the Commonwealth Scientific and Industrial Research Organization report that "both green and black tea offer protection against the sun's rays. A cup of tea may be good protection against skin cancer, possibly as good as sunscreen." Dr. Dreosti told the Medical Post that tea has high levels of a group of antioxidants that help protect cells from damage caused by ultraviolet rays. Studies at George Washington University report that too much exposure to sunlight turns off important cancer-fighting molecules on the surface of the skin.

All of us who are on immunosuppressive medication need to be particularly careful when sunbathing. I try not to go anywhere without the sunscreen I prefer most, Nivea UV Care & Daily Moisture Lotion. It has an SPF of 15, it's a light, easy-to-spread skincare lotion without any fragrance and it won't burn your eyes. A 90-ml dispenser sells for less than $10 Canadian. Consumer Reports did a survey on sunscreens based on value for one's money as well as the amount of UV protection. Bain de Soleil All-Day Extended Protection and Coppertone Moisturizing Sunblock came out on top.

Most doctors and hospitals supply you with a free booklet called "Passport to Healthy Travel," sponsored by SmithKline Beecham Vaccines, which offers a great deal of information on precautions to take when one is travelling.

— three —

Advocacy and Support Groups
and Programs for the
Transplant Patient

There are various support groups and government programs that are available to the transplant patient. Perhaps the greatest fear we all have is fear of the unknown, and one of the most important things for the transplant patient to know, both before and after the transplant operation, is that he or she is not alone. Being able to gain inspiration and guidance and friendly support from others who understand what the transplant patient is going through, because they too are in the same boat, can make such a difference in helping to boost an individual's morale. I know that I have benefited immensely from the support provided by programs such as the mentor program or the HeartLinks program at Toronto General Hospital.

The Mentor Program

After being placed on the waiting list, I was asked by Eileen Young, the senior transplant coordinator at Toronto General Hospital, if I wanted a mentor—a former heart transplant patient who would give me support and answer any questions that came to mind like a Big Brother. I gladly accepted.

My mentor was Larry Mason, a large, strong man who had had his transplant at the age of fifty-four. Larry had a good outlook on life and was very easy to talk to. The conversations we had were unlike those one would have with a doctor. I was able to ask him some very general as well as some rather intimate questions. I would often think of a detail about the upcoming operation and I would note it down for my next conversation with him. It was a great arrangement to have someone to share daily thoughts with, someone who understood.

The mentor program originated in San Diego, California, in 1990. The Toronto General Hospital heart transplant unit adopted the program in 1995 and in 1998 it was extended to the lung and liver transplant program. It was the only one of its kind for transplant patients at the time. To be a mentor one must go through a two-day training seminar. You must be a former transplant patient and be willing to support and share information. Through his or her firsthand knowledge, the mentor provides vital support to the prospective transplant patient.

Much is discussed about the psychological effect of having someone else's heart beating in your chest or any other organ in your body. It is very normal for thoughts such as, "What type of person was my donor?" "What creed or religion did they practice?" "Will it affect me or my mind in the future?"

Whenever this feeling of apprehension creeps into your thinking, try to dismiss it at once. Don't let your mind be diverted by these thoughts. My family and friends never bring up these kinds of topics. There is very little gained by dwelling on them. Be happy and grateful for the gift you have received. Take good care of it, it is your best chance for longevity.

Certainly the transplanted organ cannot transfer the personality or the background of the donor into your body. One of the first questions my family doctor asked after my operation was whether the thought of knowing that I had lost my own heart and had it replaced by someone else's would bother me psychologically. The answer was no, I felt humble, honoured and responsible to the donor's family who had had the foresight to make the transplant possible. James McLaren of Vancouver, BC, has a transplant activist Web page (http://pages.sprint.ca/transplantactivist/jamesmclaren.html) that answers a number of questions in regards to organ donation and transplantation.

———————

Transplant Ontario
(formerly known as The Multiple Organ Retrieval and Exchange M.O.R.E.)

The Transplant Ontario program was established in Canada in 1988 to alleviate the shortage of organs and ensure the full use of organs donated. It tracks organ donations in each province through its computer system, but its database does not yield key awareness, attitudinal and behavioral measures. Organ transplantation has become a highly accepted medical practice. What is needed are more donors, more people signing their donor card and making their wish known to their family.

The goals of Transplant Ontario are:

1) To meet the needs of donor families by offering to them the option of organ and tissue donation upon the tragic death of their loved one.
2) To increase organ and tissue donation.
3) To ensure the fair and equitable allocation of organs and tissues for transplant.
4) To increase public awareness and awareness among health care professionals.

A second task of Transplant Ontario is the overall purpose of research, which includes the following:

- To determine the public's level of awareness of the need for organ donation as a proven and successful medical treatment
- To determine public attitudes and participation rates in signing organ donor cards and discussing organ donations
- To determine motivational factors and barriers to participation in organ donations.

Research results are used in program development and evaluation, and in the development of corporate communications campaigns.

For an organ donor card and further information, call Transplant Ontario at 1-800-263-2833 or visit their web site at Error! Bookmark not defined. You may also get your organ donor card from any Ministry of Health and Transportation office. Make sure you sign it and carry it in your wallet.

Eileen Young, RN,
Transplant coordinator,
Toronto General Hospital

Eileen Young, RN, is also one of the original members of the Transplant Ontario. The author spoke to her about post-op care for the transplant patient.

Q: *What is the average stay in the hospital for a heart transplant patient?*

A: When we first started with the heart transplant program in 1985, we were very cautious, we would keep people in the hospital at least three to four weeks after the transplant or at least after the first three biopsies. We have come a long way and gained more experience. We became more confident. Now we let patients go home after the first biopsy, or nine to ten days after the operation. We have a rule of thumb, those who walk into the hospital usually walk out much faster. After the transplant operation we monitor for rejection and rehabilitation. If someone walked into the hospital, most likely he or she will walk out again after nine days.

Q: *You have been with the program since its inception in 1985. What, in your opinion, contributes most to the success of a transplant patient's well-being?*

A: There are physical as well as mechanical reasons. One of the problems with heart transplantation, even today with all our experience and knowledge, is that the vessel in the new heart develops blockages, and that can be fatal. But the success as to how people do has a lot to do with the emotional state of the patient. I think if the patient will follow the medical plan in regards to taking the medication on time, exercising and following a sensible diet, his or her life will be quite normal again. Report any signs or symptoms, protect yourself against excessive sun exposure. All are very basic things that are in the transplant manual.

People should follow all these things, but don't be obsessed with them. A positive mind, thinking of a second chance and getting on with life can make a big difference as to how people do.

Q: *Do you foresee a change or different way to determine heart rejection other than a biopsy?*

A: When one starts a new program, one wants to monitor it very carefully. In the past twelve years we have been doing that, but I can see the biopsy interval being lengthened. Certainly not in the first four weeks, but people get to the six-month or yearly interval much quicker than years ago. There has been a lot of research done to diagnose cardiac biopsies by echocardiogram or electrocardiogram. Perhaps down the road we will come up with a less invasive way of checking for rejection.

Q: *Why do heart transplant patients also need a heart catherization [angiogram] on a regular basis?*

A: The angiogram checks the patient's coronary arteries. We used to be very strict in doing these on a yearly basis, but with experience we learned more and now tend to tailor it to the individual person. If you had an angiogram and it is absolutely clear, we might let you go two years before the next one is done.

Q: *Is there a program coordinator for every organ?*

A: Yes, every program has a nurse coordinator. For some of the bigger programs, such as for kidney and lung, there might be two or three coordinators.

Q: *Are all or most transplant patients subject to frequent biopsies?*

A: No, the heart is the only one where biopsies are performed on a regular basis for diagnosis. In other organs, such as the kidney, the blood test or creatine level will tell if there is rejection. In liver transplants you can see the liver function test go up, and in lungs when one does a bronchoscopy you see the pulmonary function test change. But with the heart, other than a biopsy there is no other indicator.

Q: *What positive results and research have you seen in the heart transplant program over the last ten years?*

A: We have taken a more aggressive approach to preventative measures, we are now much more aggressive in giving people cholesterol-lowering drugs, in exercise rehabilitation programs, in the research of homocysteine, and hopefully all of this will make a difference. We would really like to see people back to work, travelling, engaging in interesting activities and leading a normal life. I want to clarify what I mean by saying I want them going back to work. It doesn't only refer to a paying job; many patients do voluntary work in the community or for the hospital, or work at home. It makes a difference in your life to be needed and be a productive person.

Q: *Why is there little contact or communication between donor and recipient?*

A: In order to have any communication between these two, the law would have to be changed. The Human Tissue Gift Act under which we are governed forbids us from giving any information to the donor or the recipient. I would be breaking the law by giving out such information. When the donor family signs the consent form [see Appendix II], they are assuming that it is in total medical confidentiality. The law was written in the 1960s, perhaps it needs updating. I think in some cases more information on either side could be good, but we are dealing with all kinds of personalities and ethnic and religious groups—I am not sure if loosening the law would be of great help.

Q: *The heart in my chest belongs to someone else. I represent a part of a loved one from someone's family. Would the donor family not welcome me with open arms?*

A: Yes, but what about if the donor family met you and they saw that you are overweight by a hundred pounds, or that you were an alcoholic or perhaps a smoker and you were not taking care of their son's or daughter's organ? Would you think that much would be achieved? In some cases it would be a wonderful thing, in others it could be disastrous. Should we change the law to today's standards? I am not sure if it would do any good. It is a little like the adoption laws where people want to find their real parents.

We get a great number of requests from recipients who want to know more about their donor. I don't think it is a bad idea to revise the law, but I personally wonder or have some concern as to how much damage it would do or how much benefit would it bring to someone.

Q: *The Toronto General Hospital has an "Easy Call" system [other hospitals have a similar system] for its patients, are you happy with it?*

A: The "Easy Call" works well for us and for our program. Some people would rather speak to a live person, but the problem with all the cutbacks is that we have a limited staff. The number of transplant patients is forever increasing, but not the staff. Dr. Ross and I, myself, are very busy to answer daily phone calls. We have some two thousand outpatients and not every one of them has an answering machine, a cell phone or call answer. After the clinic and after our daily review I might have twenty different drug changes to pass on to patients. To call or leave a message or write a letter is just not an economical or reliable system. People have cottages and go away in the summer or winter months and travel. They can call us from anywhere in the world and they will get their personalized message twenty-four hours a day, seven days a week. It works very well for us and the patients.

Q: *With the large number of patients to take care of, can you separate your personal life from that at the hospital?*

A: I have been a coordinator now for seventeen years. I enjoy my work and my family. One has to separate one's private and professional life. All transplant patients are part of my family, you meet them in the beginning and you are with them till death do us part. You go through all the ups and downs with them, some you get to know closer than others. When you are a caregiver, you have to know how to enjoy yourself, how to take care of yourself. I try not to take the hospital's work and problems home with me. I get very upset when something disastrous happens. I go in a corner and have a good cry and carry on.

Q: *Do you have any advice for the transplant patient?*

A: The whole key is in thinking that they have a new heart or organ, they have a new life and with it comes a responsibility to take good care of that precious gift. But don't get obsessed with that, get on with your life and live it to the fullest. We have been successful in this program and it's like with a newborn baby. Soon it gets up by itself, then it walks, and after that it runs. They need Mommy along the way. When we get people to that point, I think we have been successful.

The HeartLinks Support Group

The HeartLinks Support Group is a group of heart transplant patients and their families from Toronto General Hospital that meets at least twice each year socially, exchanges ideas and raises research funds. We meet for a summer picnic and a Christmas party.

The HeartLinks newsletter is a source of information that helps us maintain contact with one other. It gives us information on how everybody is doing, and on the latest developments in heart transplant surgery and related medication. It is an interesting publication full of the latest statistics and other reading material. HeartLinks was started in 1987 through the dedication and hard work of its members, and has become a very important part of the transplant program.

In our group we have approximately 160 heart transplant patients whose operations date as far back as 1985. The organ transplant program was started at Toronto General Hospital in 1976 with kidney transplants. The heart transplant program was started in 1985, and Bill Hofland, who passed away in February of 1999, had been our longest-surviving member as Transplant No. 002 from 1985. Bill, you were an inspiration to all of us.

The HeartLinks Support Group at annual Christmas Party

Our organization raises money by selling T-shirts and baseball caps, and we run golf tournaments and raffles as well as craft shows and sales. Our aim is to:

1) Help and provide mutual support to heart transplant patients and families, and educate transplant patients and families.
2) Promote public awareness of the importance of organ and tissue donations.
3) Address the needs and concerns of patients.
4) Raise funds for research.
5) Transmit important information to members of HeartLinks through a newsletter.

The Canadian Transplant Association

The World Transplant Games

The Canadian Transplant Association (CTA) is an organization that promotes the benefits of organ donation and transplantation through sports and community events. It was formed to motivate transplant recipients to keep fit and active and to help show the public that organ transplantation can restore people to a full and normal life. It also gives hope to those still waiting for organ donations. "A Future Is Yours To Give" is the motto of the CTA. A transplant doctor, Maurice Slapek, started the Games in 1978 in Portsmouth, England. He is the driving force behind the event and continues to tell the world that there are no winners or losers in the Games. "We are all winners in the game of life."

The Games have been held every two years in various parts of the world: New York, Vancouver, Innsbruck, Singapore, Manchester, Athens and Amsterdam, and in Budapest in 1999. The Games are competitive, but for some the participation is just for personal satisfaction. The World Games held in Hungary in 1999 were also called, "The New Life Games." Organizers wanted a name that underscored the fantastic results provided by organ transplantation. They are striving for the kind of attention that will enhance the right attitude towards organ donation. By showing transplant recipients participating in various sporting events, it will dramatically demonstrate that transplantation works and new lives are created by donations.

Sporting events such as bowling, squash, volleyball, badminton, golf, lawn bowling, the mini-marathon, swimming, cycling, table tennis, tennis, and track and field were on the program for the 1999 Transplant Olympics. If you are a transplant patient and are interested in competing or are just looking for some fun, get involved in the 2001 Transplant Olympics. Contact the Canadian chapter of CTA.

In August 2000, Sherbrooke, Quebec, hosted the first Canadian National Transplant Games. More than 150 transplant patients from Quebec alone participated, and many more came from every corner of our country. The event took place at the University of Sherbrooke, a beautiful facility, particularly for track and field and swimming.

The 2001 World Games will be held in Tokyo, Japan. Being hosts is important to the Japanese, as they have overcome decades of spiritual and medical mistrust of organ donations and recently performed the nation's first heart transplant. I am sure that these games will be a great success, not just for the participants, but for organ donor programs worldwide.

You don't have to be a superathlete to participate. All are welcome. It is an opportunity for great fellowship and the whole purpose is to bring more awareness of organ transplantation to the public. For more information and related literature, please contact:

Janet Brady, National President
Canadian Transplant Association
Phone: (519) 657-8549 or E-mail: jbrady@fanshawec.on.ca

Or write to:
Canadian Transplant Association
22 Willonwick Close, London, Ontario N6K 3Y8

Canadian Transplant Association's Dragon Boat Team.
Photo by Dick Winter

If you have access to the Internet, take a minute to check out the web site, in particular the "Forum" web page, of the Canadian Transplant Association at www.organ-donation-works.org. The Internet provides a new forum where CTA members and the community can share ideas and experiences and develop a dialogue. The membership is inexpensive: annual dues are twenty-five dollars. For membership information, corporate or individual support or sponsorship, contact:

Canadian Transplant Association
c/o Mr.Dick Winter
51 Addington Crescent
Brampton, Ontario, L6T 2R4
Phone: (905) 793-7700

The MedicAlert Foundation

With over 900,000 members in Canada and 4 million worldwide, people of all ages are benefiting from the protection of a universally recognized emergency medical identification and information service, MedicAlert. The service was established in 1961 and can be accessed from around the world, in more than 140 languages. MedicAlert offers a lifelong, comprehensive membership for those with medical conditions that should be known in the event of a medical emergency.

A custom-engraved bracelet or necklet with your own ID number displays your critical medical facts as well as a twenty-four-hour hotline number. It is a vital piece of information that should be carried on your person at all times. In the case of a medical or accidental emergency, the police or ambulance attendant is able to receive immediate information based on the MedicAlert bracelet or necklet. "Don't leave home without it."

A MedicAlert bracelet or necklet is available for thirty-five dollars, and the price includes a lifetime membership enrollment fee and an unlimited medical record update. Beware of imitations. For more information or to order the bracelet or necklets, call 1-800-668-6381.

Ontario's Trillium Drug Plan

At present, the prescription drugs I take cost me a thousand dollars per month: this includes cyclosporine, which is supplied free of charge in Ontario by hospitals, but thanks to a medical plan, in my case 85 percent of all prescription costs are paid by insurance. I am unable to quote all medications and their prices; as every case is different. One will be in good hands with the transplant doctors and transplant program coordinator regarding medication, who will assist in every other way possible.

Ontario has the Trillium Drug Program. It is a provincially generated program to assist people with lower incomes in the purchase of prescription drugs. After maximum deductions have been reached each year the plan helps pay all or part of the portion that is not covered by a medical insurance plan. Other provinces have similar programs. For instance, British Columbia has Pharmacare, a provincial drug insurance program that assists British Columbia residents in paying for prescription drugs and supplies. In Manitoba the program is called the Manitoba Provincial Drug Program, within which there are three subprograms, called Income-Based Pharmacare, Family Services Drug Program and Personal Care Home Drug Program. The Alberta Health Care Insurance Plan sponsors premium-free Alberta Blue Cross for all senior citizens in Alberta and for those enrolled under the Alberta Widows' Pension Plan. The Capital Health Authority is responsible for organ donation and transplantation in Alberta. Provincial funding for these programs comes from province-wide services. This funding covers all costs related to transplantation and medication and post-op care and is subsequently disbursed on an outpatient basis.

I made my first application for the Trillium program in July of 1997, about three months after my release from the hospital. Prior to that, I was unaware of the Trillium program and it took a few months to get all my drug receipts from my insurance company. I would show the unpaid balance of my claim. My first application and all the backup material were returned to me from the Trillium Program with a form letter that gave no name or contact person, simply telling me that the application had been turned down. After a number of calls to the Ministry of Health, I was told that my application had been received after the deadline and it could not be honoured. Nowhere in the application had there been any mention of a deadline. I explained the situation and the reason for being late, but my words fell on deaf ears. There was no compassion for my case. I wrote that year off. I made my second application at once, not to miss the deadline a second time. It came back again with a form letter telling me that I did not meet all the requirements and my application could not be processed. Again, no contact name or file number was on the correspondence. I made my third submission. Three weeks later I received a letter, this time with an application number, telling me that all I needed to do was to submit the original receipts and I would get my claim reviewed for payment. The original receipts were sent to my insurance company for partial payment, but Trillium would not accept their payment records for drugs to new receipts. The pharmacist was not very happy and muttered a few uncomplimentary remarks about the government and the Trillium program. But I finally had new hope—just one more hurdle and I would be reimbursed for the balance of my drug costs. Some three months after submitting all the necessary documents and crossing every possible "t" and dotting every "i," I received a cheque from Trillium for an amount much lower than I had anticipated.

I had understood that Trillium would pay the portion that your private insurance company would not pay, or in some cases would pay all the costs for those who did not have private medical coverage. Not so. Trillium covers only certain drugs, and for others a "Ministry Limited Use Form" must be signed by the prescribing doctor.

You must pay Trillium a co-payment or deductible depending on your income. For instance, if you paid $109.73 for the prescription and your private insurance company pays you back 85 percent, it leave $16.46 that you must pay. Trillium will pay you $14.46 and keep $2.00 towards the deductible. After you have reached your deductible, you will eventually receive a payment. The deductible varies depending on a person's income.

I have to reach my deductible, which starts new every year, before I am eligible for full payment. Once you get to the point where they acknowledge that they will give you a refund, it takes three months for the cheque to arrive.

If the government implements a program to help the less fortunate, then it should be made accessible to all, and not just to those with degrees in economics. I have written three letters to our health minister and asked that the program be simplified. I have received no reply. For further information and an application form, call toll-free long distance: 1-800-575-5386 or in Toronto: (416) 326-1558.

Revenue Canada

Clinic expenses are tax deductible. Revenue Canada has confirmed that you may claim tax deductions for car, bus, airplane or railway tickets, as well as for parking, food, accommodation and long-distance phone call expenses accrued while travelling to and from the hospital, during pre- and post-transplant care. If you travel more than forty kilometres one way for treatment, you may be able to claim these out-of-pocket expenses under the medical expense category on your income tax return form.

It is important that you state that the medical treatment or post-op care cannot be performed locally. Keep and submit all receipts for food, hotels, transportation, etc. Include a signed letter from the transplant coordinator or attending physician to verify your appointments. You can claim expenses for a twelve-month period ending in the current year.

You should also claim disability credit if you are disabled. The tax credit certificate must be completed by your doctor and included with your income tax return. The credit amounts to $4,200. For more information, call Revenue Canada at 1-800-959-8281.

— four —

A New Heart,
a New Beginning

A Second Chance

Thank you. We got a second chance.

It was very enlightening and interesting to speak to many transplant recipients and be encouraged by their success stories. There seemed to be a common bond, in that they all had a strong desire to start a new and productive life and maintain a very positive outlook to the future. Here are just a few of their stories:

Heather Fisher is the second-longest-surviving liver transplant recipient in Canada, and celebrated her sixteenth transplant anniversary in April 1999. Heather climbed Mount Kilimanjaro in 1989 to demonstrate that a healthy, active lifestyle after a transplant is achievable. She has been a medal winner, representing Canada prominently in track and field events at the World Transplant Games in Singapore, Budapest, Vancouver and Sydney. She is involved with the charitable organizations Children's Rainbow of Miracles and Partnership in Research. Heather frequently speaks to groups about organ donation and transplantation.

Elizabeth Holmberg in 1980 underwent open-heart surgery to repair a valve and an aneurysm. The surgery went well, but she never felt quite the same afterwards. In 1988, at the age of forty-five, she had to have a heart transplant. The procedure was a success and after ten years she still feels great and has lots of energy. Mary helps her husband in the operation of a ski resort near Peterborough in northern Ontario. She is convinced that her loving and long-lasting relationship with her husband had much to do with her recovery. She exercises and has a very positive attitude. Her happy disposition and positive outlook on life are her motivation for longevity.

Bob Nesbitt received a double lung transplant in December 1990. Since that time he has returned to his occupation as an engineering manager in the town of Grimsby, Ontario. Bob devotes a lot of his spare time working for charitable organizations. He has held executive positions with the Lung Association, the Canadian Cystic Fibrosis Foundation and the Canadian Transplant Games Association (CTGA). Bob is an avid curler during the fall and winter and loves to golf, cycle and do in-line skating. He has competed in the World Transplant Games in Vancouver and Manchester.

Tony Field received his new heart in 1987. It all started when he felt discomfort in his chest. Tony was driving to work from his home in Oshawa, Ontario. He arrived at the office and immediately saw a doctor. A week after that first incident he had a massive heart attack. His heart stopped. Was his life going to end at the age of fifty-three? After undergoing major heart surgery he was told that 65 percent of his heart muscle was dead. Two weeks later he suffered a second heart attack. There was only one solution—a new heart. Seventeen days after his heart transplant, Tony went home and immediately started an exercise program. He climbed 640 stairs without a break, increasing that to 4,500 steps per week. He then started a walking club at the local mall, with 820 members. Now it has become one of the largest indoor walking clubs in Canada. Each participant records his or her distance for each walk. Tony has walked the equivalent of 8,000 kilometres, the distance from St. John's, Newfoundland, to Vancouver, BC. It has been more than eleven years since his transplant and he is still going strong. He walks eighteen kilometres each day and works out on his rowing machine. Tony estimates that he has walked some 21,000 kilometres. He feels great, in spite of having only one kidney. He watches his diet, but most important of all, he has a very positive outlook. "Your mind and your attitude are very important. Be positive, don't feel sorry for yourself. Get on with your life."

Janet Brady, a keynote speaker on Organ Donation and President of The Canadian Transplant Association, speaks in elementary and secondary schools, community colleges and university medical schools about organ donation and transplantation. She is involved with two other charities, coaches children's volleyball and track teams and swims competitively. Janet received her new liver in August 1990 and exactly one year later to the day was sailing the Danube with the Canadian transplant team and captured medals in Budapest in 1991, Vancouver in 1993 and Sydney in 1997. She has also participated in the Ontario and the Miracle of Life Relay.

James McLaren is fifty-six years of age and was born in Vancouver. He is a retired sales representative. James has won championships in football, baseball and basketball, medals and trophies in track and field, and has coached football, baseball and hockey. Music is his major hobby; he plays the guitar, bass, banjo and harmonica. After twenty years of heart ailments, James received a heart transplant in April of 1996. He volunteers for the BC. Transplant Society and the Kidney Foundation, promoting organ awareness everywhere. James feels fortunate to have been able to participate in the World Transplant Games in Sydney, Australia. His favourite quote from Bob Dylan is, "I still carry with me the gift that you gave, it's part of me now, it's cherished and saved."

Bill McIlroy, a very active person who plays old-timers' hockey, badminton and golf and is an active walker, received a new heart in 1988 at the age of fifty-five. He had a heart attack the year before the transplant, which damaged his heart beyond repair. He is taking care of himself and leads an active life in Ajax, Ontario. For a while after the transplant, his pace of life slowed down somewhat, but now he is back to playing golf and walking. Bill is a keen singer and he is a member of two barbershop quartets. "I love to sing. It helps me with my mental as well as physical condition. It's good for my lungs.

"Some days I could take on the whole world. I never was, and never will be, a couch potato—I enjoy life and my activities." He has a very positive outlook and is convinced that this has helped him to get through the rough times in his life.

Tim Klassen is a living organ donor, having given the gift of life, a kidney, to his sister Melody Klassen fifteen years ago. Tim participated in the ninth World Transplant Games as a track and field coach. He is a marathon runner and an avid dragon boat racer. He coached the Canadian transplant dragon boat crew in June 1997 at the International Dragon Boat Races in Toronto, Canada. Tim is an instructor at George Brown College and is an avid promoter of organ donation. He was responsible for organizing the 1999 Canadian Transplant Team.

Richard (Dick) Winter resides in Bramalea, Ontario, is married and has two adult children. Dick received his new liver in 1990 and has been involved in promoting organ donor awareness ever since. He encourages a healthy and active lifestyle following transplantation. Dick is involved with various organizations, including the Multiple Organ Retrieval and Exchange Program in Ontario. As a keen swimmer, he represented Canada in the World Transplant Games and was a medallist in Manchester, England, in 1995.

Carol Devine was among the founding members of the Canadian Transplant Association. She has participated in all of the Transplant Games except for one. Carol lives in St. John's, Newfoundland, and received her new organ, a kidney, from her sister Brenda in 1978. She was profiled on the CBC program "Man Alive," which aired in January 1998. A number of medals at the Transplant Games can be seen in her trophy case.

Mary Markidis was forty years of age when in 1992 she received a heart transplant. She was the mother of three children, living in Ajax, Ontario, and says she was much too young to give up a future with her family. A lot of adjustments had to take place after the surgery, but today Mary is doing fine. Although her husband passed away a short while ago, her life now revolves around the children. She is a very determined lady who doesn't dwell on her past because of a very positive outlook. She plays golf three times a week and works out in the local gym. One sees that she leads a very normal life, unrestricted by medical or psychological problems. " I look at life as if I never had a transplant. I don't let it bother me or occupy my mind. I don't dwell on the past. My children are my future."

Gino Gasse had a double lung transplant in July 1989 at Montreal General Hospital. He was the first person in Quebec to undergo this kind of operation. He is married, has three children and works with the Paul-Giroux Foundation, promoting organ donor awareness and helping people with money matters, day-to-day needs or support before, during and after the operation. Gino is involved in two or three major events each year, one being a golf tournament with some four hundred participants. He is a long-distance runner in the 800m, 1,500m and 5km race. He also plays volleyball as a member of the Canadian Transplant Association's Team Canada. Gino has competed in two of the Transplant Games in Manchester and Sydney.

Linda Rowe is the founding member of the Canadian Transplant Games Association. She has been a medal winner and has participated in six World Transplant Games. Linda is a three-time kidney transplant recipient and the organ donor chair for The Kidney Foundation in Muskoka, north of Toronto. Also a regional spokesperson for Transplant Ontario, Linda organizes events to raise awareness and funds for CTGA.

Chris Dujardin married his wife Cheri two weeks before his kidney transplant in July 1993. He had waited seven years for a kidney transplant. Chris works out with weights and swims regularly. He is interested in lawn bowling and is looking forward to participating in the CTA World Transplant Games. Chris is a systems designer for a fire protection firm, is a volunteer with The Kidney Foundation and sits on the Saskatchewan Organ Donation Committee.

Kathy Tachynski was on dialysis for six and a half years before receiving her kidney transplant in 1991. She is a registered dietician and works as an administrative dietician in nutrition and food services at the Misericordia Community Hospital in Edmonton, Alberta. Kathy sings in an a cappella Ukrainian female quartet together with her twin sister. She recently sang the national anthem at a Calgary Flames hockey game. Kathy is involved with the Kidney Foundation and promotes organ donation throughout Alberta.

Jack Lamers arrived in Canada in 1953 from Holland, and has spent most of his working life in the great outdoors. Jack was a supervisor in Toronto for the Department of Parks and Recreation. His problems started with chest pains early one morning in his Oshawa, Ontario, home. He went to the local hospital and, after less than twenty minutes, Jack suffered his first heart attack right in the hospital. Things went downhill from there on. In 1988, at the age of sixty-one, Jack received a new heart but has never looked back on that time. He is content with his new lease on life and asks for very little, except a long and healthy life. The medication does not give him problems and he keeps fit by walking moderately each day. He has a great appreciation for the doctors who take care of him. "They are just great to me." His advice is to listen to your doctor's advice and follow it. "Too many people want to give you advice, but are not qualified. Have a good doctor, believe in the advice and treatment and stick with it."

Cricket Fox, from Vancouver, BC, received her kidney from one of her five siblings, who, along with their mother, all matched with her and wished to give her the gift of life! Diabetes caused Cricket's kidney to fail and she was on peritoneal dialysis for 13 months. With two other kidney recipients, she started the British Columbia division of the Canadian Transplant Games Association. She has participated in five Transplant World Games since 1989 and won medals in track events.

† **Rev. Fr. Michael A. Luchka** got up one fine morning after the '96 Super Bowl Sunday and felt the urge to shovel a light dusting of snow off his walkway. But it had been premature for him to exert himself like that. Only eight months had passed since he had undergone triple heart bypass surgery following a minor second heart attack in November of 1995. Once again, he almost slipped away into "that good night," and it must have been divine intervention when he received prompt emergency care from Larysa, his daughter.

Michael is a retired fifty-one-year-old teacher from De La Salle and St. Basil's College School and an associate pastor of St. Mary's Ukrainian Catholic Church. Six months after his heart attack, he received a new heart. In the summer, Michael plays some golf and walks his dog and goes for therapy to keep fit. He thanks God for "the three C's," Christ, compassion and competence.

† Rev. Fr. Michael A. Luchka passed away in February 2000.

Robbie's Miracle

I first met Ron and Susan Thompson at the House of Commons in Ottawa on February 9, 1999. The federal government had called upon us as expert witnesses to help Dr. Keith Martin MP, implement the new organ donor bill M-222. Ron made a very emotional plea that day in favour of a more powerful organ donor bill in Canada.

Their son Robbie, at nineteen months of age, was flown from Vancouver Island to The Hospital for the Sick Children in Toronto in September 1998. His condition had caused his heart to swell to the size of an adult's. "We got the call at 4 a.m. that day. We were staying with Robbie, he was doing very poorly, heading toward major kidney failure and unable to hold any food down." For the next while, which turned out to be a year, Sue and Ron Thompson took up residence in Toronto, with the David Foster Foundation paying for their temporary home.

When I received word of Robbie's progress from his parents, thankfully it was good news. "Finally we can send out the e-mail that we have been hoping to send for ten and a half months," his parents wrote. "Robbie underwent a heart transplant operation on Wednesday, July 21, 1999. His old heart stopped beating at 8 p.m., his donor heart started at 9:31 p.m."

Ron Thompson spoke of how, after the operation, as he and his wife Susan walked out of the hospital, they looked at each other and just talked about how incredibly lucky they were. "We will continue to work toward improving organ donation rates in Canada."

Reflecting back, Ron said, "The surgery was very successful and without any hitches. He [Robbie] went into the operating room at 5:15 p.m. and was transferred to the intensive care unit at 11:30 p.m."

Robbie's progress was amazingly quick. Less than five days after the surgery he was taking on food and drank 120 millilitres of apple juice. "But the real heroes are the family that provided Robbie's new heart. We have heard news reports that the heart came from New Jersey."

The next e-mail from Ron and Susan arrived eight days after the surgery. " Robbie is doing extremely well, he is eating all the time and starting to grow. His first biopsy showed zero rejection, we are elated and very, very lucky. There is a possibility that he will be discharged in the next week. We will be forever grateful to the donor family, their courage and selflessness has provided Robbie with an opportunity for a long, healthy life. We take a minute each day praying for them and the strength that they need during what is an immeasurable loss." On October 10, 1999, I received an e-mail from the Thompson family. "Robbie and his exhausted mom and dad are going home!!!" Fourteen months had passed since they left their home with ten-month-old Robbie, who was now twenty-one months old and full of energy. His parents' words were, "Thanks to all those who have supported us through an absolute nightmare, we are forever grateful."

A year after Robbie's transplant, Ron, his father, sent me an invitation to his first birthday after his transplant. Ron mentioned that his son is doing very well, that he and his wife just have to find enough energy to keep an eye on all his daily activities.

— • —

Not everyone who is waiting for a new heart or other organ is subjected to a lengthy waiting list. In some rare cases the donation and transplantation happen very quickly. Such was the case with fifteen-month-old Sophia Pratico from Vernon, BC. The young infant was born with two debilitating heart defects. On Christmas Eve 1999 she received a gift from God—a strong, healthy heart, after waiting only six days at The Hospital for Sick Children in Toronto. The gift came from a child she could never meet, but with whom she will forever share an intimate link.

The Pratico family has never been a very religious family. But that has changed. They were talking to a reporter three days after Sophia's transplant operation. "This sure changes our thinking. I have prayed more that ever in the last fourteen months," said her mother Sharon Pratico, a thirty-one-year-old homemaker. "It's serendipity," said Bryan, grinning as he held his daughter. "God willing that she does really well, but even if she were to go tomorrow, just to see her like that for even a day is incredible."

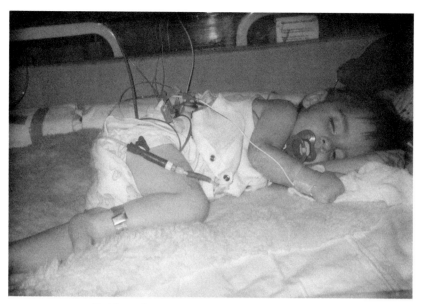

Robbie Thompson, pre- and post-transplant.

Photos by Susan Thompson

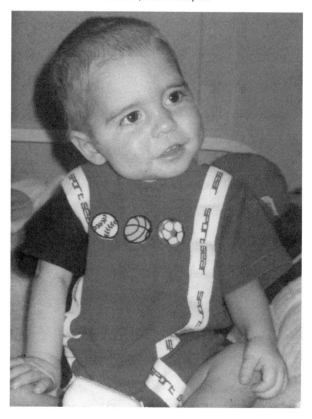

Working with His Third Heart

† *In memory of Robert Medeiros*

Is it really better the second time around? It certainly was the case with double heart-transplant recipient Robert (Robbie) Medeiros. "I had my first heart attack at the age of twenty-three. And for close to eight years I needed a daily dose of medication, but eventually the medication was failing me and I needed a new heart," said Medeiros.

Waiting for someone to die so you can live is a hard, cold fact for heart transplant recipients, but that is just one of many factors people on the waiting list have to cope with. Robert Medeiros, from Toronto, forty-three and a father of three, has twice been lucky enough to have his life given back to him.

In September of 1986 Medeiros had a heart transplant, a procedure which had been introduced in Canada only a year earlier. The medication increased to fifty pills a day to keep his new heart from being rejected and to decrease the chance of infection. "Rejection and infection are the two pitfalls for heart transplant recipients," says Eileen Young, who has been involved with Robert's case since his first heart attack in 1978. "I came into Robbie's life when he was at his worst, but throughout two heart transplants he hasn't faltered. He knows the gift he has been given and is making each day count. He is thankful to the family of the organ donor, to the hospital, to everyone. And he is giving back through volunteering at the hospital, supporting other transplant patients and through fundraising. He has not given up and never will."

And that is true. Only four years after receiving his first new heart, Medeiros suddenly became ill. He was experiencing all the signs and symptoms of a heart attack without the pain. According to Eileen Young, when performing a heart transplant, nerves are cut in the process, and that causes a lack of sensation around the heart.

"I was told my new heart was failing," Medeiros said. He was in critical condition and was again placed on the heart transplant waiting list. He was going to die if a heart did not become available in a very short time.

But in seventy-two hours, he and his family's prayers were answered. A heart became available and Medeiros was a match. "I am a lucky man," he said. "I can never repay the hospital, staff and the donor for my new lease on life."

Robert devotes a great deal of time during the summer to raising money for the heart transplant program at Toronto General Hospital. One of his projects is a 1,200-kilometre bicycle marathon in conjunction with MCpl. Denis Prud'homme and MCpl. Serge Bisson of the Canadian Armed Forces, Camp Borden, Ontario. Last year, this bicycle marathon, in which Dr. Ross also took part, raised $6,200 for the heart transplant research program.

Dr. Ross, Robert Medeiros and MCpl. Denis Prud'homme presenting proceeds from the 1,200 km bicycle marathon.

† Postscript: Robert Medeiros passed away in February 2000. He left behind many lasting memories and good friends.

The Gift of Life

Don Benson, who received a kidney from a living-related donor, has written the following:

Sacrifice of Others

"I can't help but think, as an organ transplant recipient, about the risk involved in being an immunosuppressed, drug-reliant person. The risk of picking up one of modern man's great biological nemeses, a modern virus, is more of a concern, be it cancer or hetevirus or flesh-eating virus or any of the other newer diseases we hear about daily. Because transplant recipients have a weaker bodily defense mechanism for fighting these modern diseases by being more immunosuppressed than "normal" people, it scares me to think how fragile our existence is.

"The older one gets and the more reliant one's body becomes on these drugs, the long-term effects of these drugs on one's body come into question. What limits does this put on one's life and how does this reflect the quality of one's life?

"Everyday post-transplant is important again. The intricacies and involvement of everyday life are appreciated perhaps for the first time. One's focus is not on oneself, as it has been through the course of the illness and recovery, but rather now the focus is outside of oneself. It starts, of course, with the thought and sacrifices of the donor and donor's family....The world has always had diseases and illnesses and will continue to get new ones affecting people daily. The mortality one feels is important, as each day becomes a gift. With that gift is a priority and a renewed sense of responsibility for not only our lives as transplant recipients, but for developing and continuing life around us. If life was what happened while we were busy making plans, the reality and significance of implementing and acting on those plans is now important.

"These plans go beyond personal achievement and gain, although they are important, too, but more toward an understanding of how we got this far and what we can do to maintain the importance and quality of everyone's life, rather than quantity and longevity of life."

Part Two

*T*he Facts
on Organ Transplantation

Organ Transplantation and Donation
Past, Present and Future

The History of Organ Transplants

Organ transplantation has become the treatment of choice for many conditions such as chronic kidney failure, end-stage heart disease, liver and lung failure and failure with a number of other transplantable organs. The human body offers twenty-seven tissues and organs that are transplantable. Canadians are responsible for many pioneering developments in the field of organ transplants. These include exciting work done by a Canadian, Doctor Andrew Lazarovits, on the development of a new anti-rejection medication, as well as tremendous work by Dr. Chris M. Feindel at Toronto General Hospital to help preserve the donor heart from the time of procurement.

There are also initial discussions taking place at Toronto General Hospital with a major drug company about xenotransplantation, which is the retrieval of organs from animals such as pigs and cows for transplantation in humans. Like many high-tech medical techniques, it raises a series of ethical issues. Is it the answer to our ongoing problem of organ shortage? Will animals be exploited? To the latter question the answer is yes, according to many animal-rights advocates, although there is certainly more opposition to taking organs from primates than from pigs. Many believe that pigs are the best donor candidates for xenotransplantation. Their organs are about the same size as human organs. Experimental transplants of animal organs into humans may begin next year in Britain, following applications by at least three biotech firms to the British Health Ministry.

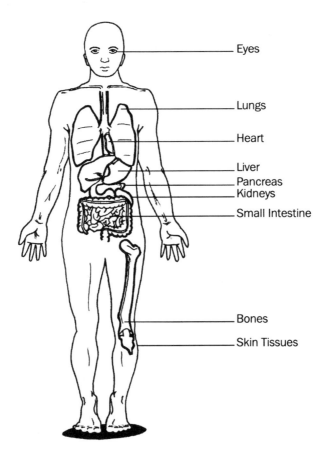

Proposed experiments include transplanting pig kidneys into humans whose own organs have failed, and injecting fetal pig brain cells into Parkinson's sufferers. The Canadian government makes the following recommendations about xenotransplantation: "All research or other activities in the area of xenotransplantation must be open and transparent to the public. As well, the Medical Research Council, and any other federal granting body, must ensure that its researchers adhere

The first animal-to-human organ transplant was reported to have taken place in 1906, when a French surgeon connected a pig's kidney to the circulatory system of one woman patient and used a goat's liver in the case of another woman patient. Though neither of these women survived, these procedures laid the groundwork for future pioneers in xenotransplantation. In 1984, the world's first modern-day xenotransplantation took place when a team from the Loma Linda Medical Center in California implanted a baboon's heart into a dying baby. The intention was to keep the infant, known as Baby Fae, alive with the baboon's heart until a human donor could be found. Baby Fae's small body rejected the organ and the child died.

Perhaps xenotransplantation may be one of the answers to our shortage of human transplantable organs—another being a government-funded public awareness campaign that will inform the people of Canada about the benefits of organ donation and transplantation.

Researchers began experimenting with organ transplantation on animals and humans as early as the eighteenth century. In the early 1800s bone marrow was first administered by mouth to patients with anemia and leukemia. Although unsuccessful, this led to multiple attempts to replace bone marrow in the following years. In 1822 the first successful skin graft (autograft) took place. In 1880 the first cases of cornea transplants were reported, and by the mid-twentieth century, successful organ transplants had been performed. In the past twenty years, important medical breakthroughs such as immunosuppressant drugs have allowed for a larger number of organ transplants and a longer survival rate. Jean Borel's discovery of an immunosuppressant drug called cyclosporine in the mid-1970s was a major breakthrough, but it took until 1983 before it was approved for commercial use.

In 1967, a human heart was transplanted into another human being for the very first time by South African surgeon Dr. Christian Barnard. Many surgeons began to adopt his procedure, but most patients were dying soon after the transplant, and the number of operations dropped from about a hundred in 1968 to eighteen in 1970. The major problem was the body's natural tendency to reject tissue from another individual.

In Palo Alto, California, Dr. Norman Shumway persisted in working on this problem, and in the early 1980s he and his colleagues could report that more than half of all transplant recipients were living beyond one year after the transplant. Although transplantation is a relatively new procedure, medications such as cyclosporine are helping to reduce the body's immune reaction to a transplanted organ or tissue.

When I asked Dr. Daly whether he has been satisfied with the progress of heart transplantation, he had this to say. "Well, we are never happy or satisfied, we are always looking for more results. Are we now further ahead and smarter than fifteen years ago? Absolutely, but we hope for many more advances to come. There is still one major threshold that we have not gotten over, which will dramatically change the way transplantation is done. It is the induction of true tolerance. The goal of true tolerance is elusive, yet there are a number of fundamental things that we don't understand about the immune system. New discoveries that look very promising and might blend in often tease us in our pursuit of true tolerances. We get teased with potentially new discoveries all the time, they get us part of the way there and seldom all the way ... "

When asked what was meant by true tolerances, Dr. Daly explained, "The major issue with all transplant patients is rejection, infection and cancer. You introduce a new protein from the harvested organ into a strange body and the immune system is unhappy or does not recognize it. We need to define that potentially harmful protein and destroy it. We need to find effective mechanisms to prevent cancer and for dealing with infection. It is basically a programming of our immune system to add to the list of benign protein strings."

Dr. Daly also pointed to several reasons why more women are entering the heart transplant program than in past years. "The mortality rate from heart failure is higher with men. Women's survival rates after transplantation are not quite as good as those of men. We now see quite a number of women in the transplant program. Women normally do not develop premature arteriosclerosis as often as men do. There are still more men developing coronary disease than women, therefore, more men receive new hearts than women."

In the HeartLinks Club, an association of heart transplant survivors from the transplant program at Toronto General Hospital, there are a number of patients who have been survivors for ten years or longer, some transplants going back as far as 1986.

On January 25, 2000 the *Toronto Star* reported on the quadruple transplant operation of a twenty-year-old man from British Columbia, Noah Kasper, who received a stomach, pancreas, liver and bowel in a

Noah Kasper, who received a stomach, pancreas, liver and bowel in a twelve-hour operation at the Toronto General Hospital. "'Miracle' is a strong word, but we know that about half the patients who are waiting for this type of transplant will die before an opportunity for a donor becomes available," said Dr. David Grant, who headed the surgical team. He said the operation, the fifth of its kind in Canada and one of just forty done in the world, has a 70 percent long-term rate of success. The problem, Dr. Grant reminds us, is that "in the City of Toronto, we're very, very poor at organ donation. It's very important that people discuss it with their family. He [Noah] is one of the lucky ones."

---

13 Transplant Operations in Only 48 Hours

A new record was set by Edmonton's University of Alberta Hospital on August 28, 2000.

Surgical teams performed a record-breaking round of organ transplants in a marathon session. In less than 48 hours they did three heart transplants, two double lungs, three liver, four kidneys and an islet cell transplant on 13 patients, all of whom recovered in the hospital's intensive care unit. A hospital official said that these transplants were the most performed in a Canadian hospital in a 48 hour span.

Milestones in Organ Transplantation

1902   First successful organ transplantation, Emerich Ullman.
        A dog's kidney was transplanted from its usual position to
        the blood vessels in the neck of the same dog. This work
        was presented to the Vienna Medical Society in 1902
        and heralded as a remarkable achievement.

1954   First successful kidney transplant. Dr. Joseph E. Murray,
        Brigham & Women's Hospital, Boston, Massachusetts.

1958   First kidney transplant performed in Canada.

1966   First successful pancreas transplant, Drs. William Kelly
        and Richard Lillehei, University of Minnesota,
        Minneapolis, Minnesota.

1967   First successful pancreas transplant. Dr. Thomas Starzl,
        University of Colorado Health Sciences Center,
        Denver, Colorado.

1967   First liver transplant performed in Pittsburgh,
        Pennsylvania.

1968   First successful heart transplant, Dr. Norman Shumway,
        Stanford University Hospital, Stanford, California.

1981   First successful heart/lung transplant, Dr. Bruce Reitz,
        Stanford University Hospital, Stanford, California.

1982   Toronto Lung Transplant Group established, Toronto
        General Hospital, Canada.

1986   First successful double lung transplant in the world,
        Dr. Joel Cooper, Toronto Lung Transplant Group,
        Toronto General Hospital, Canada.

1989   First successful living-related liver transplant,
        Dr. Christoph Broelsch.

Statistics on Organ Transplants

Miracles happen every day. However, too few people are aware of this fact. The miracle of organ donation and transplantation needs a growing number of donations each and every day to meet the demands of the future.

There are a number of organizations and government agencies, such as Transplant Ontario, the Canadian Association of Transplantation, the Canadian Institute of Health Information and the United Network for Organ Sharing (UNOS), that keep track of transplant statistics and make them available to the public. The statistics do vary slightly from one source to the next. Due to the Organ Exchange Program between the U.S. and Canada, some of the statistics may vary. Although I contacted both Transplant Canada as well as the United Network of Organ Sharing, I was unable to get much information on the actual numbers of organs being exchanged between our two countries. The following information was supplied by UNOS: In the past two years, 1998 and 1999, three hearts were received from the U.S. and we in Canada returned two kidneys, four livers, three hearts and two lungs. This is somewhat out of proportion considering Canada's population is one-tenth the size of its neighbour.

Over the past decade, there has been a 44 percent increase in the number of transplants performed, and the transplant activity in Canada continues to grow. There are seventeen transplant centres, or organ procurement centres, in Canada: five of these carry out heart transplants, seven are for kidney transplants, four deal with lung and pancreas transplantation and five do liver transplants.

In Canada, there were 429 multi-organ cadaveric donors in 1998. From these donors 1,311 organs were transplanted, involving 682 kidney, 354 liver, 176 heart, 4 heart/lung, 28 single lung, 48 double lung and 19 kidney/pancreas transplants. At the end of 1999, over 3,500 people in Canada were waiting for an organ transplant. That year, one hundred and twenty-two Canadians died while waiting for an organ. Since the beginning of the organ transplant program in Canada, over 21,000 organ transplants have been performed.

The U.S. statistics are proportionate to the population count. As of October 1997, 3,886 people were registered on the waiting list for heart transplants and some further 45,000 were on the waiting list for other organ transplants. That number had increased by approximately 521 by the end of July 1999. In 1998, there were 2,342 heart transplants performed in the United States. The United Network for Organ Sharing had a waiting list of 62,009 organ transplant patients in 1998.

United Network for Organ Sharing, "A Mission for Life"

Mission Statement:

"To advance organ availability and transplantation by uniting and supporting its communities for the benefit of patients through education, technology and policy development."

Approximately 200,000 transplants have been performed in the United States since 1954.

60,000 to 70,000 people in the U.S. have received an organ and with that, a new lease on life. Headquartered in Richmond, Virginia, the United Network for Organ Sharing is the private, non-profit organization dedicated to saving lives by marshalling the medical, scientific, public policy and technological resources needed to facilitate every organ transplant performed in the United States. Since its inception in 1977, UNOS has helped save the lives of over 215,000 people in the United States by coordinating the work of the nation's 272 transplant centers in matching donated organs with the desperately ill patients who await them.

Each and every day, an average of 56 people in the United States will get a second chance at life by receiving a transplantable organ. Currently, there are some 70,000 people all over the country that are waiting for an organ.

In 1999, although more than 20,000 people received transplanted organs, some 6,000 people died waiting for a life-saving organ. It is projected that less then half of the more than 70,000 people on the waiting list today will receive a transplant.

Every 16 minutes of every day, a new name is added to the National Organ Donor Waiting List. This country, as well as their neighbor to the north, Canada, is in desperate need of educating its people in reference to organ donation. For instance, in 1997 there were 5,478 donors; from which 20,045 life-saving transplant operations were performed. At that time, 56,716 people were on the nation's waiting list, 4,316 people that year died waiting for an organ transplant.

Share Your Life. Share Your Decision.

There are two simple steps you can take that can save lives.

1. Share your life by becoming an organ donor.
2. Share your decision with your family by discussing your wish to become an organ donor.

Remember that signing a donor card is not enough to ensure donation. You must also let your family know your wishes.

Organ Donors in Canada, the U.S. and Worldwide

	1994	1995	1996	1997	1998
Canada	412	424	434	436	429
U.S.	8,201	8,744	9,083	9,235	9,913
Worldwide	N/A	N/A	N/A	37,693	41,290

Organ Donors in 1998, by Country

	Donors	rpmp*
Austria	166	20.8
Belgium	194	19.4
Canada**	429	14.4
Czech Republic	198	19.2
Denmark	58	11.0
France	993	16.8
Germany	1,073	13.4
Italy	710	12.3
Sweden	129	14.6
Switzerland	108	15.4
Netherlands	196	13.1
U.K. and Ireland	846	13.5
United States	4,793	17.7

*Rate per million population.

**Figures given are for 1997.

Number of Organ Donors, by Province

	1994	1995	1996	1997	1998
British Columbia	41	53	47	50	38
Alberta	42	34	53	52	50
Saskatchewan	13	11	05	13	22
Manitoba	28	24	28	18	15
Ontario	147	155	161	164	162
Quebec	92	117	113	96	120
Atlantic Provinces	49	31	27	47	22

Organ Transplants Performed in 1998, by Country

Country	Cadaveric Transplants	*rpmp
Austria	674	84.2
Belgium	672	67.2
Canada	1,564	51.6
Czech Republic	509	49.4
Denmark	203	38.4
France	2,997	50.9
Germany	3,719	46.4
Italy	2,256	39.1
Sweden	411	46.3
Switzerland	360	51.4
The Netherlands	569	37.9
U.K. and Ireland	2,699	44.0
United States	16,945	62.7

* Rate per million population.

Transplants Performed Worldwide in 1998, by Organ

Liver	7,183
Heart	3,685
Lung	1,269
Kidney	24,225
Kidney/Pancreas	810
Heart/Lung	143
Pancreas	378

Organ Transplants Performed in Canada, the U.S. and Worldwide

	1994	1995	1996	1997	1998
World	N/A	N/A	N/A	57,698	49,225
U.S.	18,251	19,280	19,616	19,410	20,961
Canada	1,470	1,512	1,548	1,5	1,564

Organ Transplants Performed in Canada, by Province

	1994	1995	1996	1997	1998
British Columbia	152	138	187	188	141
Alberta	180	164	194	226	220
Saskatchewan	29	26	22	33	62
Manitoba	57	60	50	34	31
Ontario	607	635	654	627	664
Quebec	295	379	338	336	345
Atlantic Provinces	153	108	103	161	106

Organ Transplants Performed in Canada, by Province, in 1998

	Lung	Liver	Heart	Heart/ Lung	Kidney/ Pancreas	Kidney*
British Columbia	7	24	14	0	0	96
Alberta	13	56	32	2	0	117
Saskatchewan	0	0	0	0	0	62
Manitoba	5	0	0	0	0	25
Ontario	34	155	63	3	2	410
Atlantic Provinces	0	18	9	0	0	79
Quebec	17	90	36	2	0	200

*Kidney includes cadaver and living donor.

National Organ Waiting List 2000 USA-UNOS

Kidney	45,546
Liver	14,717
Pancreas	752
Pancreas Islet Cell	182
Kidney/Pancreas	1,076
Intestine	116
Heart	4,099
Heart/Lung	234
Lung	3,658

Average Waiting Time for Organ Transplants in Canada, in Days

	1994	1995	1996	1997
Kidney	805	861	964	988
Liver	136	99	103	115
Lung	179	229	298	313
Heart	116	150	148	155

In 1998 there were 3,434 patients waiting for an organ transplant in Canada.

Transplants Performed in Canada, by Organ

	1995	1996	1997	1998
Kidney*	921	952	996	998
Lung**	72	72	79	70
Liver	328	354	352	342
Heart	183	166	164	154
Heart/Lung	8	4	7	7

*Kidney includes cadaver and living donor.
**Includes single lung and double lung, as well as heart/lung.

UNOS National Waiting List for Organ Transplantation in the United States as of September 18, 2000

Type of Transplant	Number of waiting patients for transplantation
Kidney transplant	46,363
Liver transplant	16,084
Pancreas transplant	960
Pancreas islet cell transplant	160
Kidney-Pancreas transplant	2,389
Intestine transplant	131
Heart transplant	4,070
Heart-Lung transplant	221
Lung transplant	3,584
Total number of patients waiting for transplantation	71,663

Number of transplantation Performed in 1999 in the United States

Type of Transplant	Number performed
Kidney	12,483
Liver	4,698
Pancreas	363
Kidney-Pancreas	946
Intestine	70
Heart	2,185
Heart-Lung	49
Lung	885
Total transplantation performed	21,692

Number of U.S. Organ Donors by Organ as of June 30, 1999

Organ	1995	1996	1997	1998	1999
Kidney	4325	8649	8936	9498	4621
Liver	4372	4513	4657	4886	2431
Pancreas	1284	1307	1323	1462	766
Heart	2496	2476	2427	2449	1127
Lung	920	793	868	806	424
Total	8808	9123	9440	10073	4938

Above are based on UNOS statistics of Cadaveric and Living donors

Donors by Gender (living and cadaveric) in the U.S.

Donor Gender	1994	1995	1996	1997	1998	Total # of Donors
Female	3696	4134	4336	4455	4797	21,412
Male	4500	4662	4776	4929	5122	23,989

Number of U.S. Transplants by Gender from 1994 to 1998

Gender	1994	1995	1996	1997	1998	Total
Female	7463	7869	8055	8344	8598	40,329
Male	11580	12376	12448	12650	13328	62,382

Total number of U.S. Transplants performed by State from 1993 to 1998

State	Heart-Lung	Heart	Intestine	Kidney	Lung	Liver	Pancreas
Alabama	11	254	1	1765	143	468	50
Arkansas	0	128	0	609	0	0	48
Arizona	22	208	0	919	35	155	14
California	81	1637	12	8528	564	3632	579
Colorado	1	291	0	921	117	399	132
Connecticut	0	171	0	730	5	116	44
Delaware	0	0	0	12	0	0	0
DST. Columbia	0	100	0	1083	0	49	134
Florida	3	662	61	3496	119	1487	181
Georgia	1	354	0	1646	50	489	102
Hawaii	0	12	0	162	0	26	8
Illinois	14	493	9	3029	237	1271	341
Kansas	0	78	0	430	0	171	5
Indiana	4	337	0	982	103	331	38
Iowa	2	98	1	751	17	231	75
Main	0	0	0	224	0	0	0
Louisiana	0	453	3	1214	88	315	121
Kentucky	9	224	0	968	129	227	80
Maryland	1	156	1	1808	96	408	385
Massachusetts	5	386	1	2117	156	681	61
Michigan	7	292	0	2709	148	567	185
Mississippi	0	64	0	223	0	0	0
Minnesota	21	316	7	2447	195	726	554
New York	25	670	5	4284	166	1658	170
Missouri	21	531	3	1909	469	559	58
Nebraska	0	80	82	528	31	627	152
N. Hampshire	0	0	0	151	0	0	0
Nevada	0	0	0	285	0	0	9
New Jersey	0	114	0	1256	28	263	58
New Mexico	0	59	0	392	0	49	0
N. Carolina	17	393	0	1825	301	536	164
North Dakota	0	0	0	215	0	0	0
Ohio	4	741	0	3524	110	972	466
Oklahoma	0	221	1	727	26	317	17
Oregon	3	124	0	829	14	361	39
Pennsylvania	54	1344	88	4727	592	2503	417

(Continued on next page)

Rhode Island	0	0	0	89	0	0	0
Puerto Rico	0	0	0	243	0	0	0
S. Carolina	1	122	3	777	24	208	54
South Dakota	0	0	0	96	0	0	0
Tennessee	13	0	0	1775	103	415	158
Utah	0	212	0	823	34	208	50
Texas	9	1090	2	5042	333	1616	244
Vermont	0	0	0	120	0	0	2
Virginia	8	453	0	1535	164	741	116
Washington	5	203	0	1546	87	372	190
West Virginia	0	0	0	318	0	0	0
Wisconsin	4	508	3	2355	178	586	444
Total	346	13,981	282	72,144	4862	23,740	5,945

All statistics courtesy of United Network for Organ Sharing, variations are possible.

Brief Facts about Organ Donation in Ontario in 1998

- Number of people receiving an organ: 667
- Annual savings to OHIP with 10% increase of organ donation per year: $1.2 million
- Amount saved by OHIP when one patient on dialysis receives a kidney transplant: $145,618
- Number of people in Ontario waiting for an organ transplant at the end of 1998: 1,388
- Percentage of people in Ontario who say they would be willing to donate organs: 90%
- Percentage of people in Ontario who have signed a donor card: 38%

Patient Survival Rates

Patient and graft survivals were calculated using the actuarial method SAS computing language. Patient survival was computed as the interval between initiation of treatment and the date of death. Survival rates decreased substantially with age and with those with a primary diagnosis of vascular disease or diabetes:

Liver transplant: one-year patient survival rate	81%
Pancreas transplant: one-year patient survival rate	89%
Heart transplant: five-year actuarial survival rate	72%
Lung and heart transplant: one- and four-year patient survival rate respectively	75% and 60%
Kidney transplant: one- and five-year patient survival rate living respectively	98% and 92%
Kidney transplantation: one- and five-year patient survival rate, cadaveric respectively	92% and 81%

Patients Waiting for Organ Transplants in Canada, by Organ

	Kidney	Liver	Lung	Heart	Pancreas
1998	2,778	284	144	136	16
1997	2,528	248	104	128	8
1996	2,380	209	85	100	5
1995	2,126	149	43	110	4
1994	1,865	110	43	111	4
1993	1,901	65	49	91	2
1992	1,823	89	44	85	1

Patients Waiting for Organ Transplants in Canada in 1997/98, by Province

	Kidney	Liver	Lung	Heart	Pancreas
Atlantic Provin ces	206	3	1	5	0
Quebec	498	42	23	34	8
Ontario	1,004	134	29	37	19
Saskatchewan	58	0	0	0	0
Manitoba	50	0	0	0	0
Alberta	161	24	0	0	0
British Columbia	347	10	4	4	0

This total includes patients waiting for living donors as well as a combination or cluster of transplant procedures (e.g., double kidney, small bowel and/or liver, stomach, pancreas).

At Toronto General Hospital, the number of heart transplants since the inception of the heart transplant program in 1985 to the end of 1999 totalled approximately 280, and the number of survivors as of the end of 1999 was approximately 150.

Heart Transplants Performed at Toronto General Hospital

1993	1994	1995	1996	1997	1998
21	20	21	15	21	30

The majority of transplant recipients (86 percent) are aged eighteen to sixty-four. Males continue to constitute the majority (64 percent) of transplant recipients with a particular male predominance (73 percent) in heart transplants. However, this trend is quickly changing. The Toronto General Hospital reports that seven women received a new heart in 1998. There has been a steady increase in organ transplantation activity, but the increase is succeeded by the increasingly high numbers of people waiting for organs each year. There has been no change in the rate of organ donation over the last five years.

But are we making progress and are we looking for an alternative to the live heart of an organ donor? In the United States an estimated 15,000 to 20,000 people need a heart transplant each year, but there are only enough donors for about 2,000 people. The number of hearts available for transplantation is a fraction of the number of people on the heart transplant waiting list. Dr. Jacob Lavee, head of the Sheba

Medical Centre, near Tel Aviv in Israel, installed an electric pump, the "HeartMate 2," into a sixty-four-year-old patient that would function as part of the heart. Dr. Lavee said the man was on the verge of dying before the operation, his condition was critical after the fourteen-hour operation that took place on August 27, 2000. Tests after the surgery showed that the HeartMate 2 was working well. The battery-powered pump does most of the work of the left ventricle, the heart's main pumping chamber. This was the very first time this electric device was planted into a human body. "If the new technology is proven to be successful, and it will take another year, it has the potential of solving the problem on many thousands of patients waiting for heart transplants around the world," said Dr. Lavee. The doctor believes that HeartMate 2 will give a transplant patient a normal life, obviating the problem of rejection and the need for anti-rejection drugs.

It is still a little premature to start celebrating this good news considering the track record of other previously used mechanical devices. The human body does not react very favourably when a foreign object is introduced. Only time will tell if this will prove to be a viable alternative. Can you imagine the impact this could have on so many people whose lives are often hanging on the question of whether a suitable donor heart will be found in time? Perhaps the HeartMate 2 is not for everyone but it is certainly a step in the right direction in attempting to solve the terrible backlog on our waiting list.

Vital organs may be recovered and transported thousands of miles to a transplant centre for transplantation. The following are the approximate preservation times for a variety of organs and tissues.

Preservation Times for Various Organs and Tissues

Kidney	up to 72 hours
Liver	up to 18 hours
Heart	up to 7 hours
Heart/Lung	up to 7 hours
Pancreas	up to 20 hours
Cornea	up to 10 days
Skin tissue	5 years or more

Patients on Transplant Waiting Lists in North America, by Organ

	Canada			United States		
	1996	1997	1998	1996	1997	1998
Kidney	2,380	2,528	39,652	34,550	42,907	41,045
Liver	209	248	209	7467	10,629	11,349
Heart	100	148	96	3698	4,098	4,124
Lung	66	60	85	2546	2,877	3,290
Heart/Lung	100	76	14	49	240	244
Kidney/Pancreas	30	54	30	91	1463	1,784

Average Waiting Times in Days
for Transplants in Toronto, by Organ

	Kidney	Liver	Heart	Lung
1992	433	136	116	179
1993	653	99	150	229
1994	805	83	136	338
1995	861	141	112	247
1996	964	103	148	298
1997	N/A	N/A	N/A	N/A
1998	N/A	N/A	N/A	N/A

Organ Transplant Centres in Canada

Province	Number of Facilities	Organs Transplanted
Nova Scotia	2	Kidney, Liver, Heart
Quebec	11	Kidney, Liver, Heart, Lung, Pancreas
Ontario	8	Kidney, Liver, Heart, Lung, Pancreas, Bowel
Manitoba	1	Kidney, Lung
Saskatchewan	1	Kidney
Alberta	2	Kidney, Liver, Heart, Lung, Pancreas
British Columbia	3	Kidney, Liver, Heart, Lung, Pancreas

I think we must take a very serious look at our lifestyle. Heart disease is on the increase, and not only with the elderly or the overstressed, type A individual, but with the young, and particularly with the female population. One major factor contributing to this state of affairs is the tobacco industry and the fact that government allows tobacco manufacturers to operate.

Of course, our sedentary lifestyle and the diet that we are used to—mass marketed by all the fast-food giants—is not helping the cause. How long will the governments of this and all other "free and civilized countries" stand by as so many die of diseases that have been inexorably linked to cigarette smoking or exposure to secondhand smoke? The government may be fighting the growing and smoking of marijuana on every front, yet it is known from research that it is less harmful than cigarette smoking. Could the reason possibly be tax money? Marijuana is grown and produced mostly by the underground economy. They pay no taxes into the coffers of big government. It is high time that we as taxpayers demand our elected officials take a firm stand on this issue. Tremendous amounts of money is spent on health care to keep all these people suffering from smoking-related illnesses in hospitals.

Organ Transplant Research

Increasingly more research is being done to find better ways to fight heart disease and to help transplant patients live a long and normal life. The future looks brighter for these patients, with promising advances on the horizon in the field of organ transplant medicine. It is vitally important that transplant recipients and all those concerned with the advancement and success of organ procurement and transplantation, as well as with the longevity of the recipient, do everything possible when it comes to raising funds for research.

Dr. Andrew Lazarovits, a scientist at the Health Sciences Centre in London, Ontario, made headlines around the world in April 1996 with a discovery that may solve transplant medicine's worst enemy— organ rejection. He and his research team developed the CD45 monoclonal antibody, which targets and disarms immune cells responsible for organ rejection, leaving the rest of the immune system intact. Dr. Lazarovits's discovery may eliminate the need for organ transplant recipients to take anti-rejection medication.

In the fall of 1998, Dr. Lazarovits's work on this antibody was, according to him, "Moving ahead very well, thanks to the support of the Kidney Foundation of Canada and the developmental expertise of Research Corporation Technologies in Tucson, Arizona," and it was thought that it would be another year or even two before his research team entered clinical studies.

Dr. Lazarovits passed away at the beginning of 1999 and his close collaborator, Dr. R. Zhong, is continuing with the research on the CD45 monoclonal antibody.

There is also research being done to sprout new organs for transplantation, a relatively new alternative. Many researchers are attempting to grow new tissue or even entire organs for transplantation. From growing new tissue in outer space to growing bone on smart grafts to building new bladders on artificial scaffolds, the field is fast graduating from an intellectual curiosity to a tool for solving medical and scientific problems.

The prospect of transplantation of laboratory-grown organs into human beings remains years away, but this field of research is growing like never before. The ultimate goal, researchers say, is to take a small piece of a person's tissue to grow new tissue that will grow a "patch" or entire organ that is suitable for transplantation back into the patient. Such an approach would eliminate problems related to rejection, which occurs when a tissue or organ is transplanted from one person to another.

One of the most promising approaches to growing all types of body tissue relies on technology developed through the U.S. space program. Additional studies of tissue development and growth have been conducted on U.S. space shuttle missions and on the Russian space station Mir, reported Neal Pellis, a biotechnology cell science manager at the Johnson Space Center in Houston. But the biotechnology in space represents just one approach to growing new tissue and organs. On earth, researchers are working on stimulating new bone growth. "It is predicted that by the year 2007, doctors treating bone injuries will be able to pick from a hospital refrigerator a biodegradable matrix loaded with gene therapy vectors and cellular growth factors," said Cato Laurencin, an associate professor of orthopedic surgery at Allegheny University Hospital in Philadelphia. And at Harvard University, researchers have grown entire urinary bladders by attaching bladder cells to a biodegradable polymer "scaffold" that has been molded into the shape of a bladder. What will be next? Perhaps a new-grown heart or kidney?

Dr. Daly states, "There is so much new research and they are in a variety of different areas. We have looked at mechanical as well as biological solutions. I still prefer the biological solution to the mechanical one. I don't think that mechanical is the way to go, we need to understand true tolerance first. But the beauty of it is that we are closer on both fronts, mechanically and biologically, to understand true tolerance. I still believe that the biological option is by far the better solution."

Dr. Heather Ross,
Director of the Cardiac
Transplant Program

In Conversation with Dr. Heather Ross

Dr. Heather Ross, assistant professor of the divisions of cardiology and transplants and director of the cardiac transplant program of Toronto General Hospital, shared her views on the advances being made in transplant research and on other issues revolving around organ transplantation.

Q: *Are you excited about the research of Dr. Lazarovits and what do you see for the future?*

A: There is no question that this is not the only area where research is going on. There are a number of new immune therapies coming. We are going to be involved in a study this fall looking at RADB, à rapamyein derivative. Graft coronary disease is a major problem after heart transplantation. It is a very exciting time. If we can come up with a new immune therapy that deals with graft coronary disease, we should be able to extend the life of the transplant patient even longer.

In general, most new therapies are used in kidney patients before they come to the heart patient. The reason for this is that if there is a problem or reaction with a new drug used by a kidney patient, he or she can be saved by going on dialysis. With a heart patient, we may lose a life.

This is a most exciting time to be in the area of research.

This is the modern era of transplantation as opposed to the eighties, when cyclosporine just came out. We now understand so much more about the immune system that we have many more areas to target. Graft coronary disease is still a problem for us. We have other treatments for heart failure coming down the line, such as the ventricular assist system. It used to be that we transplanted somebody, knowing that we gave them five good years, hoping that perhaps the patient reaches eight or at best ten years, but knowing that on average we give everyone at least five years. That is just not good enough.

Today, knowing much more about the extra options in terms of immune treatment and learning about homocysteine and other things, the hope is that five years from now we will be saying to the patient that the average life expectancy is ten years, and not five or eight.

If I can extend someone's life by two to three years more with their own heart before they get into a transplant, then I think we have done the right thing, as long as we don't completely offset the quality of life. We need a balance between quantity and quality.

On Dr. Chris M. Feindel's side there is a tremendous amount of work looking at preservation of the heart at the time of procurement—the reason being that it will allow us to accept more hearts from further distances if we are better at keeping the heart in good condition prior to transplant.

Secondly, we know that sometimes there can be some injury to the heart while it is being stored or in transport to us. If we can prevent that, we can improve the outcome. The blood infusion is an example, it is primarily done at The Hospital for Sick Children. We have not yet done it on adult hearts. The feeling is that this new method can extend the window of time from when the heart is first procured to the time of actual transplant by two to three hours. Currently, the new heart needs to be transplanted within approximately four hours; the new blood infusion method may extend that from six to eight hours.

Q: *What about the quality of life after a transplant?*

A: In the early era of the transplant program we saw the trees for the forest. The huge oak trees standing in front of the forest were rejection, infection, graft non-function and coronary disease. We were so focused on those issues that we lost sight of the forest. Rejection is less of a problem, and infection has been much less of a problem for us because we are so much faster getting on top of it and so much more aware of what to look for. Those two trees have almost been cut down. Graft coronary disease is still an issue, but we are working on it.

Now, all of a sudden, there is that whole forest out there and that forest is that we keep these people alive and we give them a new heart and medication. But are they getting back to what is a normal life? Sexual function is an aspect of it, and we have not paid enough attention to it. The other area is osteoporosis and making sure that we are keeping people's bones happy while they are on medication. So we now have gotten past those trees that blocked our way; now we have to look at the forest and the whole transplant package in a new way.

Q: *What is the average cost of a transplant?*

A: A heart transplant costs between $100,000 to $130,000 [paid for by Health Ontario]. The cost to me is not the issue. How do you measure the cost of a saved life, or the quality of life?

Q: *Is age a barrier to transplantation?*

A: Officially, there is no age barrier in this program. But what we know from statistics published and from the Registrar is that older people do not do as well. As a consequence, when we look at somebody who is older—and I would put that over the age of sixty to sixty-five—we tend to make sure that there are no other health issues with the patient. With a twenty-year-old, we may expect something else not quite right, but for somebody who is sixty-five, that would become a very major problem. We know statistically that the outcome is not as good. In fairness, it is not that we have an age cutoff, it is an appropriate use of a very precious resource.

Q: *Why do some patients do better than others?*

A: We have reviewed our own data at length, and the reason people have died shortly after transplant is because of pulmonary hypertension [high pressure within the lung circulation]. When we talk about our 85 percent survival rate one year after the operation, almost that entire early fall-off is related to problems in the post-op period and pulmonary hypertension. After the first year, we start dealing with graft coronary diseases, which are a major problem, and we also have a problem with non-transplant diseases, such as cancer and others. We can do our best to make sure somebody doesn't have something wrong with them when we do the transplant, but things still happen.

Q: *What will the future bring?*

A: The future is why I enjoy this, there is so much that I hope is coming. This job is all-consuming. I have days when I come in my office and just close the door behind me and cry, particularly when I lose somebody. Often we are told to be more detached from patients, but I don't work that way. My problem is that I get involved. I want to believe that I can make a difference. I do have down days. But to me, the greatest single thing that keeps me going and regenerates me is my ridiculous exercise program. Things like biking three hundred miles in the Scottish Highlands. That, to me, is rejuvenation. I have my family, my dog and my friends who straighten me out if I get soft. I love this job, I would not want to be detached. When someone dies, I sit back and I review everything, I re-evaluate what could have been done differently. This is a constant educational experience.

Q: *Do most transplant patients resume a full life?*

A: Eighty percent will get back to a "normal" life, but that life still involves different medications. They can get back to their former activities. Patients need to be conscious of the fact that the heart is denervated, nerves have been cut and that they may find that they don't feel well when they first start to exercise. But they can work through that. If the patient is educated to that, then yes, they can get back to a normal life.

One of the disappointments, which in a sense I under-stand, is the unwillingness to resume work. On one hand I understand that they have a new lease on life and want to do and see as much as they can. On the other hand I would like to see more people get back to work. If the age permits an early retirement, that is just great.

Q: *What is the secret to longevity?*
A: I believe fully in the impact of an individual's faith, spirit and strength. It gives hope and strength, without a question.

Q: *Are older donors accepted in your program?*
A: We see it over and over again that the older the donor, the more likely the patient is to get graft coronary disease. That is probably because some disease is coming with the donor. UCLA used older donors for recipients. They have used older donors' hearts in patients who are less optimal candidates, and their five-year outcomes were quite reasonable. If we get better with our preservation in terms of preventing injury, that may lead to less heart artery disease, and if we get better with our immune medications, such as rapamycin and Cellcept MMF, then maybe we can extend the donor age that we will accept because we will be so much better in preventing the problem of graft coronary disease.

Q: *What is your opinion of the law in Austria with regard to organ donation?*
A: As a transplant person, I like the Austrian law. As a human being, it seems to be an infringement of an individual's rights. [Most countries in the developed world have a national network for the collection and distribution of organs. Austrian organ donor law states that a person's organs can and will be used, if needed, for transplantation upon his or her death without consent of the donor or of his or her family. The donation rate per million population (rpmp) in Austria is 25.2 compared to that of Canada at only 12.1. Belgium, a relatively small country by comparison, has a similar organ donor law, which has resulted in a surplus of organs.]

Homocysteine

"Homo" what? Just as we are getting on top of the cholesterol problem, something else comes along to make our life more difficult. Homocysteine is a naturally occurring amino acid (a building block of protein) present in everyone's blood at variable concentrations. High levels of homocysteine, which lead to clogged carotid arteries, are said to be as much a risk factor for arterial disease as high cholesterol. Numerous studies have shown that people with higher levels of homocysteine in their blood have a greater chance of developing heart disease. Studies are in the beginning stages and we probably won't know the answer for several years. Last year, for example, researchers at the Cleveland Clinic compared homocysteine levels of patients with heart disease to those of healthy subjects. High homocysteine levels more than doubled the risk for heart disease in elderly men and women. What surprised researchers the most, was that levels of homocysteine previously considered normal also put people at higher risk for heart disease. In heart transplant recipients, Dr. Steve Miner, a researcher in this field at Toronto General Hospital, has correlated high homocysteine levels with transplant coronary artery disease. Dr. Miner feels that several hurdles still exist.

1. Proper homocysteine sampling requires a dedicated lab with expertise in this field. The results you get from a family physician may not represent the true risk.

2. Once you know your homocysteine is elevated, lowering it may be a problem. In the general population, vitamins such as B6, folic acid, and B12 appear to be effective; however, these treatments have never been shown to be effective in heart transplant recipients, and different or additional testing may be necessary. Finally, lowering the levels has never actually been proven to be effective in lowering the risk of heart disease in a clinical trial. Given all of these uncertainties surrounding homocysteine at this time, your best bet is to get involved in clinical research. This will ensure that your levels are accurately measured and that you receive the most up-to-date treatment. Unfortunately, homocysteine levels are not usually tested on an individual basis and getting the homocysteine level down in otherwise healthy people can be accomplished safely, effectively and inexpensively by using vitamins.

Folic acid in doses of up to four to five milligrams a day and vitamins B6 and B12 are all effective. Natural sources of folic acid include liver, green leafy vegetables, beans, peanuts, wheat germ, whole grains and yeast. Vitamin B6 is found in meat, poultry, fish, bananas, yeast, bran and nuts, while vitamin B12 is found in liver, meat, fish, eggs and dairy products.

This finding is encouraging news for those with heart disease, for two reasons. You can order an anti-homocysteine formula containing only pure, natural nutrients, but according to Dr. Miner, artificially synthesized folic acid is actually more effective. For more information, see the August 1997 issue of "Newsweek" magazine or the January 12, 1998 issue of the *Globe and Mail*.

The Toronto General Hospital under the direction of Dr. Heather Ross and Dr. Steve Miner show the latest research studies on homocysteine levels:

In October 2000, Dr. Heather Ross reported the following finding:
"The Initial sample group consisted of 37 patients, six of whom withdrew before the completion of the study. The remaining 31 volunteers were divided into three groups. Twelve patients received folate (folic acid), 11 received pyridoxine (vitamin B6) and 8 a placebo. It was found that vitamin therapy with folate and pyridoxine lowered the homocysteine levels, but not significantly.

The second phase of this study involved an investigation of the endothelial function on the remaining volunteers of the three groups. Twenty-four patients completed this study. Nine on the folate therapy, 9 on pyridoxine and 6 on a placebo. The improvement in endothelial function in those patients on the pyridoxine therapy was significantly greater than those on the folate and placebo.

It was concluded that a supplement of pyridoxine (vitamin B6) improved the endothelial function significantly. Further research is planned to investigate the long-term effect of pyridoxine on lowering the risk of heart-artery disease."

Canada's Organ Donor System

Canada's New Organ Donor Law

Although more than 21,000 organs have been transplanted in Canada in the last few decades, one tragic fact remains: there are still not enough organs and tissues available to meet the need. In Canada, the number of organ transplants per year increased by 16 percent over a five-year period between 1991 and 1995. The number of people on transplant waiting lists in the same period has increased by 40 percent. A new name is added to the waiting list every twenty minutes, while every year hundreds of patients die waiting for a transplant.

"Unfortunately, the organ donation rate in Canada has not kept pace with the demand," said Dr. Paul Greig, chairman of the Canadian organ replacement register. Canada's donation rate remains one of the lowest in the developed world based on a rate per million population.

Austria:	25.2 rpmp*
Spain:	21.7 rpmp
Belgium:	19.0 rpmp
France:	17.0 rpmp

U.K.:	15.5 rpmp
Canada:	14.1 rpmp
Australia:	2.0 rpmp

*rpmp - rate per million population

More alarming still is that, according to an article in the *National Post*, an epidemic of liver disease will further increase the need for organ transplants by at least 500 percent over the next decade. Between 250,000 and 300,000 Canadians are infected with viral hepatitis C, which will create a huge rise in the need for transplants. But because of declining Canadian donation rates, roughly 30 percent of those 220 adults and children currently on waiting lists will die before they receive a liver transplant.

Despite all the gloom and doom, there is hope. *The Medical Post*, one of Canada's leading magazines for the health industry, states in its October 26, 1999 issue, "The wait may be over for a solution to organ donor shortages." It goes on to say, "If patience is a virtue, proponents of organ and tissue donation must be the collective Job of the late twentieth century, especially in this country, which has one of the lowest donation rates in the industrialized world."

Federal Health Minister Allan Rock accepted the recommendations in the creation of our new organ donor law. Noting that many Canadians expect action and that the important next step is a national transplant body, further work with provinces and territories is needed to develop a truly integrated and sustainable Canadian strategy. The health minister also noted that surveys in the U.S. and Spain, both of which have higher donor rates than here in Canada, reinforce the notion that our problem could be due in large part to inadequacies in how physicians and others are trained to deal with such a sensitive issue.

At present, Canada's organ donor program is so disorganized that almost one-third of those on provincial waiting lists die before they can get a transplant. Each province in Canada has its own system for organ donation and transplantation, and people who die in one province are often not considered as potential donors for patients in other provinces. There is no national database in Canada of patients who need organs, and provincial lists are often handwritten and outdated. Another factor contributing to Canada's record for donations of organs as being among the lowest amongst the developed countries, is the fact that the consent of the donor's family must be obtained before an organ donation can ever actually take place. The success rate in obtaining consent is very small compared to the need for organs: from out of 500 deaths of people who had signed a donor card, only 160 families or loved ones actually give permission for organ donation.

Contrast the situation here in Canada with that in Austria. Austria is the world leader in human organ transplants. With 44.5 kidney transplants and 13.2 heart/lung transplants per million of inhabitants, seriously ill patients in Austria have a better chance of receiving help through the transplantation of vital organs than in any other country of the world. The results are largely due to a controversial law, passed in 1982, regulating human organ transplantation and involving the concept of "presumed consent." Unless a person especially objects in advance, any and all needed organs are made available to the state for transplantation.

But let's not force the issue, we cannot compare ourselves to any European country. We are a very diverse society; we have a different mentality and we have a country that stretches some five thousand miles across. To get an organ from Vancouver to Halifax could mean a six-hour plane ride. One can cross the entire European continent in less than two hours. And Belgium and Austria have a surplus of organs for one reason only, and it is that the will of the donor is honoured.

To relieve the crisis that currently plagues Canada's organ donor system, Dr. Keith Martin, MP, from Esquimalt-Juan de Fuca, BC, introduced private member's bill M-222, which was successfully passed in an almost unprecedented show of unity through the House of Commons on October 9, 1997. "The number of people needing organ transplants far outstrips the number of available organs. This is an avoidable tragedy," Dr. Martin had declared. "In 1994 alone, 138 people died while waiting for transplants. I urge the government to draft a bill as soon as possible for the betterment of all Canadians." Dr. Martin had proposed the following:

1. A twenty-four-hour national database that would link consenting donors with the most appropriate recipients.
2. A mandated-choice strategy for possible organ donors through a mechanism, such as the federal income tax return, removing all financial disincentives that presently exist for health care facilities that are involved in transplantable tissue procurement.

3. Remove all financial disincentives that presently exist for health care facilities involved in transplantable tissue procurement.
4. Introducing legislation to protect the rights and wishes of those who consented to donate their organs.

Point number four in Dr. Martin's proposed bill is by far the most important aspect of Bill M-222. If the rest of Canada were willing to follow the example set by British Columbia, our national organ donation rate would increase considerably. When the BC registry form is filled out, it is scanned into the registry computer. When a hospital wants to identify a possible donor, they check the health card number of the patient. With that, they can connect to the registry to see if the patient is registered. If so, a fax of the signed (and legal) document can be in the hands of the doctor or nurses within minutes. It will be shown to the family as proof of their loved ones wishes to donate. You don't have to ask for consent from the family of the deceased; this legal document provides it.

Bringing in such legislation would protect the rights and wishes of those who have previously consented to donate their organs upon diagnosis of death, and would overcome a major obstacle—possible opposition from surviving family members of the deceased. In a recent poll, 81 percent of respondents indicated that if an individual has decided to become a organ donor and has signed a donor card, the family should not be able to override their loved one's decision.

However, at the same time, I take issue with the proposed use of a mandated choice strategy to enforce organ donation on unwilling citizens. After all, organ donation is an unselfish act of giving, and no one should be told or forced by legislation to make such a gift. What is needed is a public relations campaign to make the public aware of the tremendous benefits of organ transplantation. No matter how many new laws we may introduce, the only effective and realistic manner in which to increase and harvest transplantable organs is through a common sense approach. Organ donation is an act of giving that comes from the inner spiritual urge to be of help to others upon one's death. It comes from the heart. It should not be legislated by the government. This proposed bill could change our entire approach to harvesting human organs for transplantation in this country.

In November 1998, the federal health committee passed Dr. Martin's motion to study the creation of a registry, and agreed to issue its recommendations in April 1999. February 9, 1999 turned out to be a historical day in Ottawa. On that cold and dreary morning as I made my way across Wellington Street towards the centre block of the Parliament Buildings, I couldn't help but wonder who had something to do with the invasion on Parliament Hill of busloads of what seemed to me healthy, young "homeless people" who had evidently attracted the attention of hordes of TV cameras and security personnel.

The cause of all the commotion, as it turned out, was Dr. Keith Martin's Private Member's Motion M-222. It was in its final stages of reading and for the first time the committee had invited a number of organ donors and recipients to testify. I had been one of those asked to testify and give my opinion on organ donation and transplantation. One could feel the electricity in the emotionally-charged room when Ron Thompson, from Courtenay, BC, spoke. He was the father of one-year-old Robbie who was then waiting to receive a new heart at The Hospital for Sick Children in Toronto. Later one donor's mother expressed her feelings and gratitude for how professionally she was approached about the organ donation from her only son. Mr. and Mrs. Evans made a very emotional plea for a better organ donation law. They had just lost their one-year-old daughter who died while waiting for a new heart. By the end of the day, the organ donation program as well as all of its participants had made the national news.

Once a motion is passed in the House of Commons, it then obligates the government to produce a bill fulfilling the motion's objectives. If things are to proceed smoothly, a national registry could begin operating by the year 2001. On May 10, 1999, Lou Sekora, MP for the riding of Port Moody-Coquitlam, BC, tabled a second private member's bill. Mr. Sekora wrote, "The purpose of Bill C-227 is to establish a National Organ Donor Registry and to coordinate and promote organ donation throughout Canada. I believe that much more can be done in the area of organ donation. As you probably know, there is a critical shortage of donated organs in Canada. The current rate of organ donations in Canada is about 14 organs per million compared to 21 organs per million in the United States. It is my hope that Bill C-227 will improve the rate of organ donation and coordination in Canada." On October 18, 1999, this bill was introduced in the House of Commons and accepted at first reading. If Bill C-227 is deemed to be a passable and doable item, it then goes into committee study and onto the order paper for up to three hours during its second reading and debate in the Commons. After that, it will go to a third reading in the Commons before going to the Senate for approval. The aim is to have this new law in effect during 2001.

But when this passes into law, will we be adequately prepared for such a change? Will our hospitals be capable of handling an overload of harvested organs, organs that at present are going unused? Will the hospitals have the room for additional post-op for transplant patients who all need intensive-care facilities for the first few days or weeks? Or are we facing a new challenge that is beyond our means? Instead of acquiring more organs for transplantation, we are creating more and more expense from the health care budget. The two are a time bomb about to go off. At present, we can't perform three lung transplants in one hospital without running out of room. Should we encourage a greater effort to collect more organs or focus on upgrading our intensive-care facilities first?

The future of Canada's organ donor system looks brighter than it has in the past. But although this new legislation will help address certain problems in the current system, at the same time it will raise other issues to be resolved. We may be on the path to much-needed reform, but it is a path still laden with potential pitfalls. On October 15, 1999, Canada's health minister, Allan Rock, responded to the recommendation on organ and tissue donation and transplantation in Canada made by the standing committee on health.

"Many Canadian families came to the standing committee with stories about how organ donations can change their lives," he said. "They have told us that they expect action in response to the standing committee on health's report. An important next step will be the establishment of a national transplant council and further work with provinces and territories to develop a truly integrated and sustainable Canadian strategy for organ and tissue donation and transplantation."

Health Canada is now working with provinces, territories, health care professionals, ethicists and other interested parties on a business plan for a transplant council that was reviewed by the federal and all provincial health ministries in November 1999. This plan focused on key areas such as:

- the designations of critical care units in each province and territory whose mandate will include responsibility for donation,
- the development of common safety standards for organ and

tissue transplantation,

- reporting requirements for hospital services with respect to organ and tissue donation and transplant activity and,
- the development of a comprehensive public awareness strategy to assist individuals in making personal decisions about organ and tissue donation.

"The issue of organ and tissue donation is a very personal one—and it is a decision that all Canadians must make for themselves, and share with their families and loved ones," said Rock. "As government, our role is to put in place a comprehensive system that enables Canadians to make their wishes known and ensures that those in need can benefit from the donations that are made."

But why is it taking so long for this much-needed bill to be implemented? How many more people need to die needlessly on our nation's organ waiting lists just because our elected government officials are dragging their feet rather than implementing the will of the people?

On October 21, 1999, Ontario premier Mike Harris announced in his throne speech at the opening of the Ontario Parliament the appointment of colourful hockey commentator, Don Cherry, as official spokesperson for a campaign to double the organ donation rate over the next five years in Ontario. Cherry's son Tim, at fifteen, had received a kidney donation from his twenty-two-year-old sister Cindy. "Doubling is going to be tough, but I guess you shoot high," were Cherry's comments. The throne speech outlined the development of an "Organ Donor Action Plan" to raise public awareness through outreach and education. "We all can save lives by filling out organ donation cards and advising loved ones of our intentions so that they may honour our wishes."

Unfortunately, there was no announcement made as to the amount of government funding that would be available for this campaign. When I contacted Organ Donation Ontario, the governing body in that province, about Don Cherry's role for increasing organ donations, I was told that they were never contacted prior to or after the announcement. Upon questioning Premier Harris on this point, I received the following reply. "Mr. Don Cherry was chosen to chair the Advisory Board both for his personal experience with organ donation and his longstanding interest in this cause. I am pleased to see that these recently announced initiatives have already raised the profile of organ donation significantly. The Ministry of Health and Long-Term Care is currently reviewing what resources are necessary to meet our objective of doubling the organ donation rate by 2005."

The current system is not perfect, as this next story will reveal. Twenty-year-old Shara Quinn and her friend, Stine Olsen, died on December 28th, 1999. Their car collided with an Ontario Provincial Police car near Orillia, Ontario, due to severe weather conditions. The friend Stine was killed instantly and Shara was transported to the hospital. In the girl's personal belongings, the police found their wallets and identification. While Shara was rushed to the Orillia hospital, her organ donor card and other ID was held by the OPP. She died on the operating table, with the fact that she had signed an organ donor card remaining unknown.

Her father, Jim Quinn of Collingwood, Ontario said, "The system fell apart at all levels. Neither the hospital nor the OPP had the foresight to try to find out if she wanted to be a donor. They wouldn't have been prepared even if the organ donor card had made it to the hospital and they had been aware that she wanted to be a donor. Rural hospitals are not set up for organ procurement. They would have had to call Toronto and have a harvest team come to Orillia, but in order for that to happen, they would have had to know her wish. They could have used her tissues and cornea after the fact, at the very least, but again with rural hospitals this is not a part of their practice. We had contacted the hospital regarding their policies on organ/tissue procurement and were told that their record is dismal and they are not set up for it.

"At the time we were too shocked to remember her wish and did not think of it until many hours after her death. This is probably the case with many families involved in a sudden death. The decision/ thought should not be left to the family at this horrendous time. A system should be in place so the opportunity to help save lives does not get missed. We feel this was a total waste of potential organs that could have saved lives. The frustrating part is that we had a donor, but the system blew it. We can't help but think of the thousands of people waiting, not knowing whether they will have the opportunity to live or be missed. I can't imagine being a parent on the other end of this dilemma, waiting for an organ to save my child's life, it would drive me insane."

Her mother, Madeline recalls that, " Shara was a really caring and concerned person. She made friends easily and worked hard on keeping up her friendships. She was the one that was always worrying and looking after everyone. She had a really good heart. Shara first discussed organ donation some six months before the accident. She was renewing her OHIP card and an additional form was provided for organ donor consent. She discussed it with her mom and decided it was a good idea. The organ donor information was printed on the magnetic strip on the back of the card. This was not visible to the OPP who investigated into the accident nor was it passed on to the hospital. We aren't even sure if a magnetic reader at that time was available at the hospital. We also realize that the primary concern of the OPP and the hospital was to take care of the girls, which we are grateful for but feel so much more could have been achieved from this loss.

"I still have a very romantic attachment to the heart," said her mother. "If her heart had gone to someone else, there would have been a little part of her still with us. Knowing her organs could have helped five or six other needy people, would have been a real comfort to us."

Shara's father commented, "The frustrating part in Shara's case is that she made it alive to the Orillia hospital, she could have been on a ventilator until the procurement team arrived. I don't understand it, the whole thing about organ donation fell apart here. The donor card and the hospital never connected. I firmly believe that there should be a national registrar similar to BC, where they can find out in minutes whether someone is a registered donor that would take care of these missed opportunities. The OPP and the rural hospitals need to have better procedures in place to be able to handle this life and death issue."

Needless to say, Shara's parents are very upset because of this tragic oversight. The irony of this story is that this young lady had made a valuable decision to donate her organs and with that wish could have given new life to others, but the system failed her.

Some new headway has been made as far as organ donor consent: On February 22, 2000 the Aurora OPP held a news conference for a very special effort on their behalf. They named it, "Shara's Song," OPP Inspector Ted Rathwell and Superintendent Jay Hope initiated a program whereby province wide the OPP and their families would unite to sign their organ donor cards. At the time of the news conference 100 OPP officers and 150 civilian employees had signed their cards with the potential of thousands more. Unfortunately the conference did not receive any headlines. Transportation truckers were blocking the major highways objecting to high gas prices, so the newsworthiness was lost.

As well, the Collingwood area Kinsmen/Kinettes decided to promote the signing of organ cards throughout their club, which nationwide would number in the thousands. Organ donation ties in very much with the Kinsmen/Kinettes whose major fund raising concern is Cystic Fibrosis (CF), a deadly lung disease in young children. To date Kinsmen/Kinettes nationwide have raised over 25 million for CF research. Also neighbors and friends of the Quinns have come to realize the need for the signing of their cards which prior to Shara's death some mentioned they had not given any thought to. Out of this tragedy and oversight some awareness and good has come.

New OHIP cards being distributed by the province very clearly state on the back: DONOR/DONNEUR. The province also issues a printed organ donor card that should be in everyone's wallet at all times. It is also wise to carry an extra organ donor card in the glove compartment of your car. Cards are available by phoning Transplant Ontario, or when you first obtain or renew your drivers licence, you can have the Ministry of Transportation mail you an organ donor card or you can receive one from Organ Donation Ontario at 1-800-263-2833.

Shortly after the Quinns' tragic accident, Premier Mike Harris announced better coordination would be the central component of a plan to double the province's organ donation rate, with step one being the formation of a new advisory board on Organ Donation. I applied and offered my help and expertise but was never contacted.

On Thursday, July 13, 2000, Premier Mike Harris announced at The Toronto Hospital for Sick Children that he was determined to double the province's transplant rate within the next five years. To achieve this, the government would increase annual funding for organ donation from the current $47 million to $120 million by the year 2005. New legislation is to be tabled later this year. It would be followed with recommendations from the premier's advisory board on organ and tissue donation. "The long arm of the law is not going to get involved," Harris said during his visit. "It will be individuals first and family members who will always have the last say and I haven't seen anything in the recommendations that is in any way intrusive." He went on to say that too many people in Ontario are dying while waiting for organ transplants, including fourteen patients at that hospital the previous year.

The current system in British Columbia and Nova Scotia calls for any death or imminent death to be reported to an agency that would then determine if the deceased was a suitable donor. Specially trained hospital staff and experts would contact family members to inform them of the benefits of organ donation. Premier Harris insists that organ donation will always be a decision for the families to make, that it will not be forced on them by the government. "A large and important part of this is to encourage family members to talk about this now, today, while people are healthy."

The province will create the Trillium Gift of Life Network, an agency that would coordinate organ donations if the legislation is enacted. The network would include an education program that puts organ donation information into the high school curriculum. Failure to obtain consent has been blamed for Ontario's low donor rate. In comparison, the Atlantic provinces have a rate of 19.5 for every million. In Ontario alone, 1,720 residents are waiting for organ transplants. Last year, 617 of the procedures were performed, and more than 400,000 people are currently in the registry.

Ontario Premier Mike Harris teams up with Don Cherry and transplant recipient Seth Delguidice and his mother to boost Organ Donation.

Photo: Boris Spremo, courtesy of the *Toronto Star*.

Organ Donation Based on Religious Grouping

It has been said that charity, in its purest and most honorable form, occurs when one stranger passes along a gift to another. It is a particularly touching scenario when a personal tragedy is turned around through the science of organ and tissue transplantation to bring renewed life and hope for others.

Organ donation is a sensitive topic with a number of religious groups. In a Canadian city such as Toronto, where there is a tremendous diversity of ethnic groups, the acceptance of organ donation and transplantation varies greatly from one religious denomination to another.

Transplant Ontario has conducted an extensive study of three religious groups in the Chinese, Muslim and Jewish communities.

Here is a short excerpt from information provided by Transplant Ontario:

First consider the statistics: Becoming an organ donor is not based on race, creed or religion. It can save or change as many as twenty-five lives per donor. Yet only a small fraction of the population is donating organs. Each year in Canada approximately 6,000 people die who could be potential donors. Yet, only about 400 actually provide organs and tissues for the 1,600-plus transplantations performed every year.

It is important to discover the barriers that hinder organ donation in the Chinese community. Common reasons for lack of consent include, "fear of premature termination of life support, inability of the family to accept the death of their loved one, no knowledge of the wishes of the deceased, religious beliefs and fear of mutilation of the body of the potential donor."

Even in the Chinese community there is more of a chance that someone will need a transplant than there is of someone becoming a potential organ donor. The broad-based messages are not successfully reaching members of this fast-growing multicultural population in Ontario. In North America, ethnic minorities have low rates of organ donation. Ways must be found to reach this diverse audience. The Chinese population in Ontario is an important group to target for organ donation. The Greater Toronto area has grown more than 70 percent in the past decade and now numbers over 100,000 Chinese.

The Muslim constituency in Canada continues to become more

diverse and medical technology continues its advance, organ donation among the Muslim population may be increasing if Muslim community leaders were to encourage organ donation. Islam encourages life-saving medical treatment for all diseases. Saving a life is a noble act; taking a life is a form of murder. This would include inappropriate and false declaration of brain death. The great majority of Muslim jurists, Sunni and Shi'a, rule that organ donation for purposes of treatment or cure of chronic disease is permissible. Islam stresses the importance of prompt burial of the body, and ideally all body parts should be buried with it. But the all-important question is...how long can one take and not give?

Cultural issues are less likely an influence on attitudes of younger Muslims. Older Muslims are more willing to donate to family members first, then to other Muslims in need and then to another person in need. On the other hand the survey showed that 83 percent of all Muslims would be willing to accept an organ for treatment or cure. Muslims would be more willing to donate as well if they were made aware that the process of signing donor cards is very simple.

It has long been recognized that members of the Jewish community do not generally sign organ donor cards or consent to the donation of the organ of their family members, despite the fact that most rabbis and other Jewish scholars support the practice of organ donation. In all groups the most commonly cited reason for not signing was a belief that the Jewish religion forbids such an act. A significant number of respondents indicated that ethical concern and fear of inadequate medical care for potential donors were also important reasons for not signing donor cards. Most Rabbinical authorities now sanction organ donation for transplantation, yet some concern still exists. One major concern that was raised by rabbis was a fear that the donor's body will not be treated with dignity. Because the synagogue is such a valuable asset for increasing awareness about organ donation, it is important that rabbis are prepared to deal with this sensitive issue. It is a great relief for everyone on a transplant waiting list to know that even some of the reluctant groups are now sharing interest.

In the January 6, 2000 issue of *The Canadian Jewish News*, Henry Charles Cowen, Vice-President of the Canadian Transplant Association, Ontario region, wrote in an editorial, "I praise Rabbi Reuven Bulka for his involvement and excellent efforts as chair of the organ donations committee of the Kidney Foundation for Eastern

Ontario, and his opinion regarding Jewish organ donations. I hope and pray that what the worthy rabbi indicated in the article will open the door for organ donations from the Jewish community. I plead with you to please come forward and help all those, young and old, who are badly in need of organs for transplantation. Trust me that the lists are long, and people are dying before organs are made available to them. We say, "He who saves one life is as if he saved the whole world." Let's do it and soon.

Three main conclusions can be drawn from these Transplant Ontario studies on cultural attitudes toward organ donation:

1. Education is a significant determination of attitudes toward organ transplantation.

2. That a gap exists between awareness, willingness and donation behavior.

3. That this dichotomy cannot be explained by the lack of awareness of organ donation issues.

Frequently Asked Questions about Becoming an Organ Donor

Many questions come to mind when considering or being confronted about organ donation. Transplant Ontario makes available excellent material that will answer your questions:

How do I arrange to donate my organs after death?
The most important thing you can do is let your family know what you want. Sign a donor card, discuss it with your family and get their assurance that they will respect your wishes. A signed donor card is a legal document that allows for organ donation. Doctors, however, have respect for families' feelings and will not retrieve organs if there are objections.

Couldn't I just include it in my will?
No. Organs must be retrieved as quickly as possible after brain death has been declared. Wills are generally read long after death has occurred and by that time the organs could never be used.

How do they decide who can be an organ donor?
The patient must be in the hospital, on a ventilator and declared brain dead by two physicians who have nothing to do with transplants. Brain death is defined as total cessation of brain function as manifested by the absence of consciousness, spontaneous movements, absence of respiration and of all brainstem functions, and occurs after head injuries or head traumas such as strokes, aneurysms or bleeding in the brain. Just one to two percent of all deaths are brain deaths. No one is "too old" to donate organs. The health of the organ, rather than the age of the organ, is considered. The oldest organ donor in Ontario was ninety-two years old.

How long does it take to get the body back to the family after organ donation?
Donor coordinators at the transplant centres try to make and complete all arrangements within twenty-four hours. The time is needed to set up retrieval teams, book an operation for both organ retrieval and transplantation and contact the recipients and their doctors. If death occurs in a hospital unable to do organ retrievals, the body may be

moved to the transplant hospital. There may be unavoidable delays in trying to get everything organized, but donor coordinators will keep the family informed of their progress. They understand that the family wants to proceed with funeral arrangements and will do everything they can to assist them.

Will it affect the actual funeral arrangements?
Funeral plans can proceed as originally instructed even if there was organ donation. If the family wishes, an open casket funeral can be held. The donor is treated with respect and dignity in the operating room and no one will know that donation has taken place unless the family shares that information.

If I donate organs, will my funeral cost be covered?
The family handles funeral costs as if organ donation had not occurred. The Ontario government covers the charges incurred if a donor body has to be taken from the community to a transplant hospital. If a family is charged for the transportation of the body in this case, they should immediately send that portion of the bill to Transplant Ontario and the family or funeral home will be reimbursed.

Can I donate my organs, then give my body to medical science?
Whole body donation is different from organ donation. Whole bodies are used for education and research at schools of anatomy. They will not accept a body when organ donation has taken place, as they need the whole body. If you are considering whole body donation, contact the nearest school of anatomy, fill out an application and let your family know.

Where can I get a donor card?
If you drive, you will receive a separate donor card when your licence arrives in the mail. It will be in the cardboard folder. If you don't drive or need more cards, contact Transplant Ontario.

Can financial contributions be made to Transplant Ontario by a loved one in my memory?
Yes. Transplant Ontario, is a registered charity. Charitable donations are used to further education among health professionals and the public. Receipts and acknowledgements are issued. The majority of

funeral homes in the province have the cards and memoriam envelopes available. You can also phone 1-800-263-2833 and make a donation on your VISA card.

Can I pre-plan arrangements for my funeral?
Yes. Organizations that help you make these types of arrangements exist. One example of a funeral pre-arrangement organization is The Pre-Planning Network.

How can I receive more information about the donation process?
All the arrangements that allow the organ donation process to occur are handled by coordinators at Transplant Ontario. These co-ordinators will be happy to answer any questions you may have before, during or after the donation process. They are available twenty-four hours a day. Please contact them if you have any questions or concerns. But most of all, we need you; please consider signing your organ donor card.

Kimberly Young is president of the Canadian Association of Transplantation (CAT). Here are also some of the questions she is asked most frequently regarding organ donation:

Q: *According to public opinion surveys, most people support organ and tissue donation. Yet we hear every day of people on waiting lists dying because of a shortage of organs and tissues for transplant. Why can't the need for organs and tissues be met?*

A: One critical reason for the shortage of organ and tissue donors is that potential donors may be missed because their families do not know their loved one's wishes. A 1996 survey showed that 54 percent of Canadians did not know their family's wishes regarding organ donation. Consequently, when families are asking to consider donation after death has occurred, they are unsure about their loved one's wishes and agonize over making the right decision. In some provinces a printout of your wishes from the donor registry would be available; however, in other regions where the hospital does not initiate or follow the discussion with the family regarding organ and tissue donation, donation may not occur. Another reason is that to be an organ donor, brain death must occur.

Q: *What is the success rate for organ transplants?*

A: It varies depending on the organ, but in general, the success rate for transplantation is excellent: between 70 to 95 percent of recipients are doing great one year after surgery.

Q: *Who can be a donor, and assuming someone had made clear their wish to become an organ donor, what's the process to act on that wish?*

A: A person who becomes an organ donor invariably dies following a severe brain injury. Brain damage is so extensive that the whole brain dies as a result of insufficient blood and oxygen. Once brain death occurs, the body will die and organ donation may proceed with the consent of the donor's family. If your family is not aware of your wishes, it may be difficult to act on your behalf.

Q: *What happens after the organs and tissues have been retrieved?*

A: Funeral arrangements need not be changed. And if the family so chooses, an open casket is still possible. The names of organ recipients cannot be legally provided to donor families, but many recipients and their families wish to contact donor families to express their gratitude. Letters from recipients are forwarded to donor families by transplant program co-ordinators. These valued letters often help donor families who grieve over the loss of their loved one.

Q: *What organs can be donated?*

A: Every organ donor can help save or improve the lives of many people. The organs that can be donated are the kidneys, heart, lungs, liver, pancreas and bowel.

Q: *Who can donate tissues and what tissues can be donated?*

A: Tissue donation is possible with any kind of death. Major infections and history of cancer are the two most common reasons why donations cannot occur.

Tissue transplantation enhances lives by restoring function, promoting healing and providing vision. The tissues which can be donated are: eyes, bone, skin, heart valves and veins. Tissues may be stored for months.

Q: *Does my signature on a donor or registration card guarantee that my organs will be used for transplant?*

A: No. Your signature on your donor card symbolizes your willingness to donate, but the ultimate decision regarding donation rests with your family. Make them aware of your wishes in order that they can act on your behalf. Also, all organs are not medically suitable for transplantation. This is determined with the assessment of the donor done after consent by the family.

No matter where in Canada, your wish to become an organ and tissue donor can be displayed on your health care card, driver's license, donor program card or registration card. If you decide to become an organ and tissue donor, be assured that your gracious act will touch the lives of many.

Organ donation provides perhaps the only opportunity for something life-giving to come out of the tragic death of a loved one.

Q: *How does one become a donor?*

A: The closest family member of the deceased must sign consent for donation at the time of death. The most important step for anyone who wants to be an organ or tissue donor is to make this decision beforehand and to discuss it with his or her family. Signing an organ donor card is one way of making a wish to become a donor known, but it is vitally important to tell family members of your decision. Prior knowledge of your wish will enable the family to follow the wishes of the deceased.

Organ donation occurs during that short period of time between confirmation of brain death and the end of all organ function.

Important Organ Donor/Recipient Facts

- In the United States alone, nearly 60,000 people are waiting for organs, and in Canada, where the number is proportionately smaller, about 3,100 people are on the waiting list.
- Twenty-seven organs and tissues, including lungs, kidneys, hearts, skin, corneas and arteries, can be harvested for transplantation.
- The health of the organs and tissues is more important than the age of the donor. Acceptable organ donors can range in age from a newborn to sixty-five years or more, and successful heart transplants have been done using organs donated by people older than eighty years of age.
- In 1996 nearly 4,000 Americans and approximately 1,500 Canadians died while waiting for a transplant.
- Only 12,000 to 15,000 people declared brain dead each year can donate organs in the U.S. In 1996 alone, 5,416 became tissue or organ donors, compared to less than 400 in Canada. It's no wonder that Canada rates amongst the lowest organ donors in the world.
- In Canada alone, at any one time, more than 3,500 people are on waiting lists for transplant operations that could either enhance or save their lives.
- For every patient in Canada who receives a heart transplant, six others are waiting.
- There are approximately 70,000 deaths in Ontario in any given year. Five hundred of these, or 0.7 percent, would be suitable as organ donors (i.e., 1,000 kidneys, 500 hearts, livers or lungs being available for transplant). Out of these 500, only 160 donors per year actually transpire.
- Ninety percent of people in Ontario are willing to donate organs of loved ones, 38 percent of people in Ontario have a signed donor card and less than 1.2 percent have actually donated organs for transplantation. The donor rates from 1991 to 1997 have fluctuated between 14.4 to 14.8 per million population in Canada.

- In Canada, transplant operations have a success rate of between 85 and 95 percent.
- Studies have shown that a vast majority of donor families find consolation in their decision to donate.
- In the U.S. more than 36,000 patients are waiting for an organ transplant. Less than half of these patients will be transplanted; about 2,000 new patients are added to the waiting list each month.
- About one-third of the patients who are on the list for heart, liver, and lung transplants in the U.S. die while waiting because of the lack of available organs.
- Every day, about eight to nine people die in the United States while waiting for a transplant of a vital organ, such as a heart, liver, kidney, pancreas, lung or bone marrow.
- About 12 percent of patients currently waiting for liver transplants are young people less than eighteen years of age.
- In the U.S. an estimated 10,000 to 14,000 people who die each year meet the criteria for organ donation, but less than half of that number become actual organ donors.
- Another person is added to the national waiting list in the United States for an organ transplant every sixteen minutes.

Make Your Wishes Clear

Transplantation is a true miracle of modern medicine. The heart, lung and liver of one donor can provide renewed health and longer lives for three people. Their kidneys can save two more people many tedious hours of dialysis treatment. Many of us would want to provide these gifts to restore health to people who are critically ill. "If I knew that Shara's organs would have made a difference to someone else's life, I would feel so much better," said Madeline Quinn, whose daughter was tragically killed in a car accident.

When you have made your wishes clear to be an organ donor, please talk to your family. It is much easier for them to act on your behalf in an extremely stressful situation. Most families who have donated their loved one's organs say that the donation has helped them find comfort in a tragic situation.

Five ways that you can talk to your family about organ donation:

1. Look for a suitable opportunity to talk about organ donation.
2. Make your personal decision about organ donation known to your family.
3. Talk to them where and when it feels natural and comfortable to all.
4. Have your discussion with everyone who may need to know and make the decision.
5. Find out what each person would want to say when asked for permission from medical staff.

Silent Heroes

The organ donation and transplantation process is made up of two separate but equally important entities: people who donate organs and the patients who receive them. Each and every day, somewhere in the world someone or some family donates a loved one's organs. We, the recipients, are unaware as to whose they are and from where they come. The organ donor law in Canada does not permit the recipient to know the donor's name or to make contact with his or her family. Perhaps it is the best way for both parties in order to maintain a peaceful existence.

The TV news media generally takes very little interest in the stories of these anonymous donors who allow people like me to continue carrying on a full and meaningful life. The media is preoccupied with sport celebrities, stories of crime and natural disaster or the latest gossip about Hollywood celebrities. It shows little patience for the silent heroes who make our lives a much better place to live. Perhaps, when there is a slow news day, an organ donor or recipient may get a few seconds of airtime. If it were not for small-town newspapers or the occasional wire service picking up on these heroic donor stories, we would probably never know about them.

Only in the last two years have government agencies and politicians put forth any effort to change the situation. A number of silent hero stories will help everyone to better understand the crisis in the organ donation system.

The MOD Squad

Here is a new and unique idea that originated in upstate New York. MOD stands for Mothers of Donors, in which the mothers of organ donors assist families in the decision-making process about organ donation when faced with the death of a loved one.

This upstate New York organ procurement organization has found that when mothers who have donated their children's organs assist trained professionals in requesting consent for donation from others, the consent rate increases dramatically. In 1997, the Center for Donation and Transplant, at the Albany Medical College in Albany, New York, initiated a program called the MOD Squad. Members of the MOD Squad are women who have faced the death of their own children, and responded by giving the child's organs for transplantation. Their aim was to do their part by helping to increase the organ donor rate.

After receiving the appropriate training from medical staff, the women accompany organ procurement teams when they meet with families of potential donors. The MOD Squad provides comfort, counseling and information about organ donation. According to a press release from the Albany Medical Center, recent data show consistent benefit, with 32 of 36 families approached by MOD Squad mothers ultimately agreeing to donate. The press release notes that the average consent rate in the United States is approximately 50%.

At the 27th International Congress in Rome the results of MOD Squad's first 22 month in existence was reviewed. Twenty of the 22 families with whom the MOD Squad was involved ultimately consented to organ donation, for a consent rate of 91%. During the same period, transplant coordinators working without the MOD Squad had a consent rate of 55%. In September 2000, the MOD Program received a federal grant of $783,882. With this help, the program expanded throughout upstate New York with volunteers being recruited in Syracuse, Rochester and Buffalo.

Many states and provinces are requesting and receiving increased founding for the much-need organ donor program. For instance, Premier Mike Harris of Ontario has allocated some 20 million dollars to increase Ontario's organ donor rate within 5 years by 50%. This is certainly a great shot in the arm. The MOD Squad is by far the best, most effective and sensible way to increase organ donation in a dignified humane way. There are numerous mothers, fathers and family members that have gone through the ordeal of donating organs from a loved one. They have experienced the gratification and inner peace this gift can bring to others. Let us unit in these common concerns, to increase organ donation in our countries. Let us follow the footsteps set by the MOD Squad. Any parent or family member of an organ donor, who is interested in this project, please contact the writer.

Step by Step—The Canada 500 Day Walk

"Upon awaking from surgery, I clearly remember two things: thanking God for another chance at life, and praying for the family that was grieving that night because they had lost a loved one. Yet, amidst their grief they made that courageous decision to save the lives of others and mine was one of those lives that was saved. I wanted to say 'thank you.'"

These were the words of George Marcello in 1993 after he received a liver transplant at the Toronto General Hospital. I first met George some 115 days into to his "Canada 500 day walk." It was a beautiful fall day in Collingwood, Ontario near my hometown. I was asked to join George as we walked down Hurontario Street. I was amazed with the reception he received and also with the generosity of the spectators along the streets when we passed by. George had left Toronto's City Hall on June 20th, 2000. Mayor Mel Lastman said goodbye and good luck to George by lighting his "Torch of Life," an authentic Olympic torch that he carries with him along his route of 500 cities and towns across our great country. The purpose of the walk is to double the rate of organ and tissue donation in Canada. It is also to educate the public about organ donation and to raise funds for research on how to best increase the rate of organ donation.

"I just can't live in a country that is next to last in anything in the world. I feel the urge to due my part after I received a new lease on life." Collingwood mayor Terry Geddes was very impressed and visibly shaken by this young looking 44-year-old. "Don't get into detail or I just break down with tearful emotions," were the mayor's words. After the usual photo ops and receiving a warm welcome, a hat and a certificate, the mayor made a $ 50 contributions on behalf of the town. George and his crew of 4 were on their way again. Before leaving he said, "I can't sing, or dance, or write, so I thought, why not walk!"

The route will take George through Ontario, Manitoba, Saskatchewan, Alberta and British Columbia, he then will fly to Newfoundland and walk through that province as well as Nova Scotia, Price Edward Island, New Brunswick, Quebec and finish back in Toronto by December 2001.

George is also the co-founder of "Step By Step" a non-profit charitable organization Reg.#87933 2427 RR000, which is dedicated to increasing the rate of organ and tissue donations in Canada. For further information, help or contributions call 416-658-3936 or www.stepbystep.ca.

Mayor Terry Geddes of Collingwood, Ontario with George Marcello and Madeline Quinn with Olympic torch, June 20, 2000.

Photo: N. Hoferichter

A Sheriff Launches Organ Donor Initiative

Another example as to what can be done if citizens all work together.

"In the past year, more than 80 Louisiana residents died for lack of an organ donation," Caddo Parish Sheriff Don Hathaway said in launching a local donor program. " More than 900 Louisiana residents waited for life-saving organ donations in the past year, but there were only 88 donations to meet this critical need. Tragically of the 812 citizens who continued to wait, 10 percent of them will die."

The National Sheriffs Association (NSA) has established the "gift of Life Foundation" to enhance national awareness of the need for organ and tissue donations. The Caddo Parish Sheriff's Office has joined the NSA, the Louisiana Organ Procurement Agency (LOPA), the Louisiana Donor Registry (LDR) and other parishes across the state to encourage deputies and citizens to help with this vital program.

"We have made presentations encouraging deputies to consider becoming organ donors," the Sheriff said in announcing the initiative at a news conference. "So far, we have signed up some 30 new donors."

Mickey Mantle's Family Sets Up Organ Donor Program

Mickey Mantle's family set up a program to honor the baseball legend's final wish—to promote organ donor awareness. Since Mantle received a liver transplant, the national registry on organ transplantation in Richmond, Va., have doubled, says spokeswoman Esther Benenson. Of more than 41,000 patients on waiting lists, more than 17,000 are women, nearly 24,000 are men. The majority, almost 24,000, are between the ages of 18 and 49; almost 1,500 are younger than 18. In 1994, 3,097 people died while waiting for a new organ in the United States. Of the possible 12,000 would-be donors in 1994, the number of donors has been approximately 4,500, it went up by 300 donors the year after.

Dash for Organ Donation Awareness

More than 2,000 runners and walkers took part to increase organ and tissue donation at the forth annual DASH for Organ Donor Awareness. The Delaware Valley Transplant Program, organizer of the DASH (also know as "Gift of Life"), market their 25th anniversary as the region's organ donor program.

DASH has raised more than $90,000. Money raised will fund more donor awareness events and education programs throughout the region of southern New Jersey, eastern Pennsylvania and Delaware. Funds will also be used to fund the U.S. Transplant Games.

Friends and family of DASH enjoy live music, face painting, clowns, balloons, and information posters as the participant await the start of the 10 km run and 3km walk.

Ryan's Hope and Courage

In April 1999, I read a story that at first sounded too good to be true. What I mean is that all the pieces fit so perfectly, it had all the makings of a well-constructed campaign by an advertising company for organ donation. I let it slide for a while and on April 28, 2000 Rosemarie and I attended the 6th Intra-Denominational Memorial Service in honour of the organ and tissue donors and their families at St. Michael's Cathedral in Toronto. Dale and Nancy Doige of Aurora, Ontario, were on the speaker's list that evening. After their very eloquent and touching presentation, I realized that the story I read in April 1999 was not something a PR person had imagined, but something perfectly true.

Ryan Doige was intrigued when he saw his father Dale filling out the organ donor card that came with the renewal of his driver licence. When Ryan learned from his father that organ donation could save a person's life, the ten-year-old encouraged his entire family, including his grandmother, to sign their organ donor cards. Approximately one month later, in May 1997, Ryan suffered a massive cerebral hemorrhage. After being rushed to the hospital, he was declared brain dead.

Asked if they'd consider donating Ryan's organs, his parents answered together, "Oh yes, our son would have wanted that." Nancy, the boy's mother, said, "To be faced with that decision in a moment of crisis would be very difficult if you never talked about it. We want to encourage people to talk about organ donation at home. It was so simple to Ryan and it made so much sense to him. We've always taught him when you die, your spirit goes to heaven and you leave your body behind."

If someone at the age of ten understands the process of organ donation so well, why can't more adults have the same courage and understanding?

Ryan's organs, the corneas, kidneys, pancreas, lungs, liver and four heart valves were donated and shared amongst seven people. The recipients included those listed below.

- A twenty-year-old male university student who regained sight from one cornea.

- A thirty-year-old woman who received Ryan's kidney and pancreas.

- A sixteen-year-old boy with cystic fibrosis who received Ryan's two lungs.

- A six-year-old girl who is no longer on dialysis after receiving a kidney.

- A forty-two-year-old woman who received Ryan's liver.

- A young person who regained his sight after receiving Ryan's second cornea.

"Knowing how much it's done for someone else, it does give a bit of comfort. It brings a bit of joy," Ryan's mother said.

The Aurora couple made a monumental decision when they agreed to donate Ryan's organ. The Toronto Hospital for Sick Children recognized them with a fitting award.

Nancy and Dale Doige are very active in the Organ Donation Program in Ontario. They just recently shared a task force and TV news conference with Premier Mike Harris of Ontario, to encourage greater organ donations in Ontario by the year 2005.

Dale and Nancy Lee Doige, with Jamie and photo of Ryan.

Photo: Mike Slaughter, courtesy of the *Toronto Star*

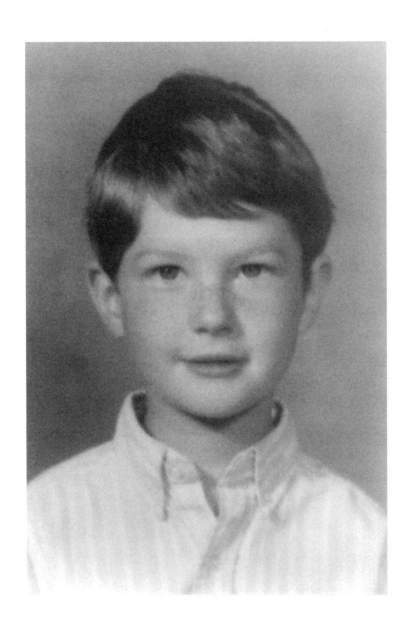

Nicholas Green

Photo courtesy of the Green Family.

When Reg and Maggie Green's seven-year-old son, Nicholas, was shot and killed by would-be robbers during a family vacation in Italy in 1994, the Bodega Bay, California couple donated his organs to Italians in need of transplants. "In a country with one of Europe's lowest organ-donation rates, the gesture was almost too generous to comprehend," went an article written in "People" magazine in its twenty-five-year anniversary issue, of March 1999. Nicholas' Gift, the moving television documentary on the Green family's life-affirming story, aired on CBS in April of 1998, starring Jamie Lee Curtis and Alan Bates. USA WEEKEND also featured a very moving article written by Nicholas's father entitled, "From a Child's Death, the Gift of Life."

Here is the family's story, in the father's own words: "The head of the intensive care unit at the Polyclinic Hospital in Messina, Sicily, stood silent in the sunlit room with his team of doctors, waiting for us to sit down." Then, gently and without preamble, he said, 'Mr. and Mrs. Green, I have bad news. We can find no sign of brain activity in your son.'

"It was what we'd dreaded for two days, since Nicholas, just seven years old, had been shot in the head by highway robbers during our vacation in Italy.

"Are you sure?" my wife, Maggie, asked quietly.

"Yes, but we'll do another test," he replied.

"She and I sat close together, holding hands at times, saying little, but feeling already the bleakness of spending the rest of our lives without him.

"Forty minutes later, they came back with the results. Still nothing. A wonderful mind that had been crammed with dreams and high ideals was empty, and I knew I could never be really happy again. As we tried to absorb the impact, one of us—we don't remember which—said, 'Now that he's gone, shouldn't we donate his organs?'

'Yes,' said the other. There was no discussion. It seemed so obvious. His future had been taken from him; now the future could be given to someone else.

"It turned out to be the future of seven people: a nineteen-year-old girl who was dying as we sat in that room; two parents going blind, one a mother who had never seen her baby's face clearly; a diabetic who'd been repeatedly in comas; two youngsters who had lost their childhood to kidney disease; and a fifteen-year-old, boy who was wasting away in a hospital, and who was no bigger than a seven-year-old received Nicholas's pure heart.

"On that day three years ago, these people were just statistics to us, some of the thousands around the world who die every year because there aren't enough organ donors anywhere. But knowing them, as we do now, and learning of the pain and fear they had gone through, it's clear that if we had made a different decision, we never could look back without a deep sense of shame.

"From the start, the attack itself—at night, on the main road from Rome to Sicily—had been front-page news and led to the biggest manhunt in Italian history. The police were baffled; the only theory they came up with was that the attackers had mistaken our small rental car, with its Rome license plates, for one making deliveries to jewelry stores.

"Our decision to donate turned intense public interest into a firestorm. Everywhere we went the media and crowds of people surrounded us with tears in their eyes. The president and prime minister asked to meet with us privately; streets, schools and playgrounds all over Italy, and the country's largest hospital, has been named for Nicholas—and organ donation rates there have doubled.

"The slaughter of an innocent lit a spark of love in millions of hearts. Beside hundreds of letters from people, who want to say something comforting, we've seen articles in, among other languages, Chinese, Russian, Portuguese, Arabic and Polish. It's known as 'the Nicholas Effect,' and it means perhaps thousands of people are alive because of his example.

"It doesn't take away the emptiness. Nothing I do seems complete anymore. But it does help when I remember that, even in the act of dying, Nicholas saved others in desperate need when no one else could."

"He was the most giving child I have ever met," his first-grade teacher, Loretta Smith, has said of Nicholas. "I always knew he was my teacher. But I had no idea that this friendly little boy who walked into my classroom every morning would be a teacher to millions. It's an epitaph a great man might envy."

Turning Tragedy into Triumph

Something good had happened that day…. It was just a month after Christmas on a sunny, mild day; a typical January thaw in Perth, Ontario. Donna Marie and her husband Bryan had just finished some shopping and were walking along the main street. He was holding their seven-month-old daughter Jenna-Marie in his arms, giving her little pecks on the cheek every few steps.

CRACK!! is all they heard. The next thing Bryan remembers is being on his hands and knees and seeing Jenna-Marie, in her pink snowsuit, lying on her back about six feet in front of him. He looked behind in panic and saw his wife. She was lying on her back, blood coming out the side of her mouth, still holding the grocery bags. Bryan's immediate thought: an atomic bomb. When he looked around, all he could see were big chunks of ice (the coroner's inquest estimated it at half a ton).

A nurse walking on the other side of the street rushed to help. An ambulance whisked Donna-Marie and Jenna-Marie to the Perth War Memorial Hospital. The attending physician told Bryan his daughter had a large haematoma (a bump on the head) and his wife had a concussion. He told him he wanted to send Jenna-Marie to the Children's Hospital of Eastern Ontario and admit Donna-Marie for observation.

Bryan accompanied his daughter to Ottawa. Once there, she underwent a CAT scan. The results of that test revealed a small fracture to the base of her skull. The neurosurgeon told him not to worry, his daughter would be fine, and that he should return to Perth and attend to his wife. He complied.

The phone call came at 2 a.m., just like in the movies. It was the neurosurgeon, and he told Bryan that he needed his consent to perform emergency surgery. Jenna-Marie's brain had started to swell and he needed to relieve the pressure. Consent was given.

The operation lasted seven hours and saw them having to remove the entire front portion of Jenna-Marie's brain. Jenna-Marie had just started to walk. Understandably, their first question to the neuro-surgeons went something like this, "Would she ever walk, talk or even know them?" Their answer, "We don't know." They were facing every parent's worst nightmare. They remember pinching themselves in hopes of walking from this nightmare. To them this was like the stories they read in big city newspapers, not in The Perth Courier! Before retiring that night the neurosurgeons had asked them what they wanted them to do in the event their daughter had a cardiac arrest during the night, a likelihood based on the extent of her injuries. Bryan and Donna-Marie, in consultation with family members, agreed to let nature take its course.

They retired to Ronald McDonald house. It was difficult for them to focus on anything except their daughter's plight. Bryan and Donna-Marie equated it to being in a dark, windowless room. They felt so helpless with so few options. Bryan could not think, he heard little of what the physician said. There was little hope for Jenna-Marie's survival, while Donna-Marie focused on hope.

Bryan remembered Donna-Marie recounting a news item that she had seen on a Toronto television program. It involved a little girl by the name of Lindsay Eberhart and focused on a public appeal to find her a liver. He recalls his wife's saying, "If worse was to come to worse, maybe we should donate her organs." This became the turning point of their tragedy. If they could not change the circumstances of their tragedy, they were going to do their best to triumph over someone else's.

The next morning Bryan and Donna-Marie went to the ICU and found Jenna-Marie, lying lifeless, connected to many life-support machines. They approached the attending neurosurgeon and mentioned their thoughts of organ donation. Bryan recalls the expression on one of the surgeon's faces as of one who just had a thousand-pound brick removed from his shoulders and quotes him as saying, "We wanted to approach you but we just didn't know how." The rest is history.

Jenna-Marie Margaret Bowers died in the early morning of January 26th. The light: Three lives were given a second chance. Jenna-Marie's liver went to a young boy in Texas and her kidneys went to children in Ohio and New York.

The Bowers believe that organ donation gives meaning and purpose to human life.

—•—

In 1997, the Erb family made the decision to donate their four-year-old son's organ. Kathy Erb talks about the impact of that powerful choice.

"My husband and I decided to donate our son Logan's organs because we knew he was gone. If we could save another person by doing that, we knew what we needed to do.

"I think organ donation is something that you need to look at and make a decision about. It helps a great deal; it helps with the grieving process, too. With Logan's organs going on, I think more positively than I do negatively. I have more good days that bad."

When asked what message she would like to send to people who are not yet organ donors, she responded, "A lot of people think that having the pink sticker (used only in the U.S.) on their driver's license is enough, but you need to let your family know. It's helped us every day knowing that there is a little girl alive because of Logan, that he's living on in someone else. We've had communication since it's happened, and we're hoping to meet her."

—•—

Theresa Ross, of Carleton Place, Ontario, speaks of her own experience of donating her father George's organs when he died in 1997 at the age of forty-eight from a stroke. "When I was eighteen, my father passed away very suddenly. My family had never discussed organ donation before that day, but we decided we wanted others to benefit from our loss. For me, the decision ended up being the only positive aspect of my dad's death. The day after he died, we received a phone call from the transplant program coordinator telling us that our choice gave five individuals a better chance at life. That was truly a beautiful feeling, knowing that even though we were hurting, we were able to brighten the future for five other people and their families.

"The decision to donate my dad's organs also made my family realize how important it is to discuss organ donation with your loved ones. Since that time, we've all sat down together and talked about our fears and wishes around organ donation. Make your decision about organ donation and take the time to talk to your family about it."

As Pat Scherbin of The Multiple Organ and Exchange Program explains, "The reason for donating varies from person to person. They need to make it clear to their family and relatives under what situation they want to be maintained on life support and under what situation they do not."

—•—

In my research and during my interviews with donor families, I saw the overwhelming sense of gratification and love that the act of organ donation had brought to those left behind by the death of a loved one.

Reg Green, the father of seven-year-old Nicholas Green who was killed in Italy, declared, "For the rest of our lives, we donor families can feel proud that our loved ones saved someone when no one else in the world could." Kathy Erb, the mother of Logan, said, "It helped us every day knowing that there is a little girl alive because of Logan, that he's living on in someone else."

Bryan Bowers had this to say. "I can remember feeling bad because we were feeling good when we thought we should be feeling bad. Couples who lose children due to accidents fall within a high percentile for separation or divorce. I credit the ability of being able to donate our daughter's organs for rendering those statistics insignificant in our lives. Organ donation in fact enabled us to move forward. Today we have three children, Bryson, Trent, and Elyse a family that collectively rejoices in a renewed life, thanks to organ donation."

Dianne Dalton, whose son was killed while in the U.S., said, "Our experience with organ donation was so positive that we began speaking out and letting as many people as possible know how important it is. It also helped us tremendously with our grieving."

I have not spoken to or heard from any donor family whose experience of donating had not been a very positive one. Yes, there are the odd rumours floating around about regrets or mismanagement by the donor's hospital, but they are nothing more than rumours, usually hearsay from a second party.

Honouring Our Organ Donors

"If Chris doesn't make it, could we donate his organs?" Maurice Dalton had asked his wife as he was looking at his son in a Pennsylvania hospital room.

"It seemed to be so right at the time," recalled Dianne Dalton, Chris's mother. "It had to have been divine inspiration." Chris was still alive, but his very serious head injuries gave him very little chance for survival. The doctors had tried everything they could but without success. At 7:30 a.m. on October 28, 1996, Chris was pronounced brain dead. He was only twenty-seven years of age.

"At 3:30 p.m. on that day, we were called to see our son's body," said Mrs. Dalton. "Chris had been treated with the utmost care and dignity." Chris had given the ultimate gift, the gift of life.

Since Chris's accident had occurred while he was in the U.S., the organs were donated in that country. In the spring of 1997 his parents were invited to attend the Organ Donor Recognition ceremony being held in Washington, DC. Transplant Ontario, with the Delaware Valley Transplant Program, made it possible for the Daltons to attend this wonderful and inspiring weekend seminar and ceremony.

Maurice and Dianne Dalton at the 1997 Organ Donor Recognition
Ceremony, Washington, D.C.

Vice-President Al Gore presented Mr. and Mrs. Dalton with a National Donor Recognition Medal. They made these comments after the ceremony. "Our lives have changed forever. We will always speak out about organ donation and how important it is. We are thankful that Chris was able to be an organ donor and we will never let him be forgotten." Chris was able to save the lives of five people. A sixty-eight-year-old grandmother received his lungs, a forty-eight-year-old man received a new heart, a forty-year-old man got a new liver and two people each received a kidney.

Upon their return to Canada, the Daltons began lobbying on behalf of the London, Ontario, Health Science Centre and Transplant Ontario. Their plea was that we, in Canada, should start to recognize our organ donors in an appropriate or similar way

Across Canada, on certain dates, usually in the spring, we celebrate Organ Donor Awareness Week. In Ontario it's celebrated from April 18 to 24. It is a time to reflect and be thankful to the donor and the donor family, to be thankful to the medical staff and doctors, and most of all to be thankful to the Lord.

A memorial service at St. Michael's Cathedral in Toronto is part of this celebration. It is a non-denominational service where both the donor families and the recipients gather together. The appreciation for the service and the deep-felt urge to say thank you to donors in this way is shown by the ever-increasing attendance each year. In its first year, the service attracted about one hundred and twenty-five people. At last year's service, more than a thousand were present.

The Hospital for Sick Children in Toronto awards the Gift of Life Medal. It was created by the Canadian Association of Transplantation and the Canadian Transplant Society to recognize living donors and donor families who made the decision to donate the organs of a loved one so that another could live. In April of 1999, the medal was presented to ten organ donor families.

Pickering, Ajax-Whitby Liberal MP Dan McTeague, would like to see April 21 of each year set aside as a day to honour organ donors such as two-year-old Stuart Herriott, who died on that day. "Every year there are literally thousands of people who are giving the gift of life," McTeague said. Eventually he would like to see a monument on parliament hill listing the names of all past organ donors. "There's so many people out there with stories like this. You never think when you sign the donor card you could donate your child's organs."

Mayor Jack Burrows of North Bay, Ontario proclaimed April 20th to 26th of each year as National Organ Donor and Tissue Awareness Week in his city.

Reed Elley, MP for Nanaimo-Cowichan, British Columbia, has introduced a private member's bill entitled, "Awarding of the Organ Donation Medal Act." Mr. Elley commented at a press conference in April 1999, "Throughout the recent months, the standing committee on health has listened to many witnesses on organ donation. During this process it has been apparent to me that there is a need to recognize and honour the individuals who have ensured that someone else's life would be healthier and richer."

In Toronto, April 19th to 25th was designated Donor Awareness Week by The Canadian Association of Transplantation, which supports and promotes organ and tissue donor awareness. All three major newspapers in Toronto gave the Organ Donor and Transplantation Program a big boost by running a full-page article with colour photographs of transplant recipients signing a giant donor card. Mayor Mel Lastman took time out of his busy schedule to address the two hundred attendees at the event.

The largest Organ Donor Thank You card at Toronto's City Hall.

Photo: Jim Wilkes, courtesy of the *Toronto Star*

Sheila Hutchings, whose teenage daughter Kathleen was killed in a car accident, was among the attendees. "My daughter would have been thrilled and honoured. That was her destiny, to carry on through someone else." At least five people—recipients of Kathleen's liver, kidney, heart, valves and corneas—found hope and a new life through the young girl's tragedy.

"Figure skater Hillary Schieve wants to get her hands on your organ," said an advertisement. Hillary had been a U.S. national figure skating medallist and a kidney recipient. She created the world's largest organ donor card to raise national awareness. The campaign centrepiece, a huge organ donor card, has room for fifty thousand signatures—a number representing the number of Americans who are waiting for a life-saving organ every year. The figure skater is embarking on a worldwide campaign with the slogan, "I want to get my hands on your organ," and has been seeking endorsements from everyone from Howard Stern to Hillary Clinton.

"People need to realize that this cause has a cure," says Schieve. Former Toronto Raptors forward Carlos Rogers joined the campaign and was the first name added to the card. The NBA player had recently lost his sister Rene Rogers, twenty-eight, while she was waiting for a kidney transplant.

How about taking up the challenge, Canada, and creating our own huge donor card or National Donor Recognition Medal?

Clinton Administration Launches National Organ and Tissue Donation Initiative

Vice President Al Gore and HHS Secretary Donna E. Shalala launched a initiative aimed at reducing the number of Americans who die each year while waiting for an organ transplant.

"Too often families choose not to donate simply because they haven't had a discussion to determine their loved one's wishes," Vice-President Gore said. "We want this initiative to encourage more families to have these dialogues to understand their loved ones' wishes and help save lives."

"Organ transplant techniques today are saving and improving thousands of lives every year, but not enough organs are available to help everyone in need, and more Americans are dying while awaiting an organ transplant," Secretary Shalala said. "We are missing thousands of opportunities for donations every year. We need to do better."

An estimated 10,000 to 15,000 death in the U.S. each year could result in organ donation. However, there are now only about 5,500 donors each year. A study in 1996 showed that 32 percent of families agreed to donations; 36 percent of families denied consent for donation. About 4,000 Americans died in 1996 while awaiting an organ transplant, this up from about 1,500 in 1988. The number of cadaveric organ donors each year has increased from 4,084 in 1988 to 5,417 in 1996. Despite the increase in donors, deaths among those on the organ donor waiting list have grown from 1,507 to 4,022 during the same period.

The Vice-President announced new joint efforts with the national Coalition on Donation. "This is a message all Americans need to hear and understand," Secretary Shalala said. "Just signing a donor card isn't enough. You must tell your family."

On September 24, 1999, Vice-President Al Gore held a discussion about the importance of organ and tissue donation, and announced several major developments, including a major new public service advertising campaign and a $13 million grant program designed to increase donations, as well as an Organ Donor Leave Act. All these are aims to reduce financial disincentives to living organ donation by enabling federal employees to use up to a week of leave to serve as a bone marrow donor, and up to a month to serve as an organ donor.

What if we in Canada were to take up the challenge and match the efforts of our friends south of the border? If our leaders, our government, would stop spending so much taxpayers' money toward armaments of destruction and put some of it towards something more life-affirming. What a difference it would make if only a small portion of the vast amounts of money collected every year from lottery revenues, for example, was put towards supporting a nationwide public awareness campaign for organ donation.

Canada's health care system is thought to be one of the best in the world, but at the same time, Canadians are being left in the dark as to the inadequacy of their health care system in addressing the ever-growing gap between demand for organ transplantation and a constant scarcity of supply—matters that could affect themselves, their loved ones, or someone they know. Unfortunately, most Canadians have not been made aware of the true dimensions of this crisis in their health care system. Raising public awareness is a key factor, and it is evident that we in Canada have a great deal to learn from the proactive measures being initiated in the U.S. to raise public awareness on the issue.

Saying Thank You

Dear Heart Donor Family,

On February 5, 1997 I received the gift of life, a new heart. Due to your generosity and God's willingness, my life is now renewed.

It is with great regret that it was to have taken something from your loved one to allow me to carry on. I hope that the satisfaction of knowing you have given the gift of life to someone else will strengthen you in your belief as well as in your daily life.

God works in rather mysterious ways, much too complicated for we humans to understand. Your donation must bring you inner peace and satisfaction as to the Lord's workings.

I will pray for you and your loved one in the hope that you will go through life knowing that the correct decision was made. God bless your family.

Yours, forever grateful,
Heart recipient

— • —

How do you repay someone or say thank you for the gift of life, a new organ? It takes a very special person to have the foresight to sign a donor card. It takes an even more courageous family to allow the donation of organs to happen. It brings comfort, and even joy to the donor's loved ones, in those dark hours, knowing that his or her last wish was fulfilled and that through such unselfishness someone else's life is saved. Organ donation can provide the only opportunity for something life-affirming to come out of the tragic death of a loved one.

The transplant recipient is not told who the donor is, whether that person was male or female, or anything of their age, creed, religion or cause of death. The name or address of the donor are not given. However, there are exceptions. *The Toronto Star* of October 24, 1999, carried the headline "The Champion, the Miracle and the Legacy." It reported the story of the late Olympic swimming champion Victor

Davis, the gold and three-time silver medal winner, who was tragically killed in Montreal in a car accident. Victor Davis carried an organ donor card and his father, Mel, agreed that his organs should be donated. The article, ten years after Victor's death, identified the four recipients of his organs. His heart had gone to a fifty-one-year-old painter, Claude Jacques, who is alive and well in Montreal. "I was able to see my two grandsons born," Jacques was reported as saying in the three-page article.

The organ recipient is encouraged to send a letter of appreciation to the donor family through the transplant coordinator. But at no time is the name or address of the recipient to be given. It is the only way to conduct the matter properly, although in my case, I know that I really did feel a strong desire to meet the donor's family and thank them for my new life.

Victor Davis celebrates his Olympic win.

Photo: Jeff Goode, courtesy of the *Toronto Star*.

I am not generally a procrastinator, but when it came time to writing my letter, I found every reason and excuse to delay it. I just could not get myself to sit down to write an intelligent letter to my donor's family without breaking in tears. But I valued the opportunity to express my gratitude. I wanted the letter to have meaning and be open to my true feelings. For weeks I agonized over every word, and the process advanced very slowly. Five months after the transplant, I finally felt that I was ready. I was overcome with a great sense of urgency to sit down and complete the connection to the donor's family.

There is no right or wrong time or particular way to write to the donor's family. It depends on your mental and physical state after your transplant. It is very important that the letter is completed as soon as you feel mentally strong and capable enough of undertaking the task of denoting your true feelings.

I delivered the letter to my transplant coordinator who, in turn, passed it on to the donor's family. The hardest part is knowing you will never receive an acknowledgment. But deep down, you know it can bring peace and happiness to the donor family.

The number of transplants done in Canada and the United States increases by a very small margin each and every year, yet that number is simply not keeping up with what is needed, with the urgent demand for suitable organs for transplantation. There has been very little change in the rate of organ donation for the past five years, and the waiting list continues getting longer and longer.

Organ donation is based on the kindness and generosity of a donor and the support of their family. Complete a donor card and carry it with you at all times. Make sure your family is aware of your desire to donate your organs. It that can bring new life to someone in desperate need.

A letter written to a donor family by a woman who received a new liver and a new lease on life. Her words express the deep gratitude that all organ recipients feel; the impact of receiving an organ donation can have on another human being's life.

—•—

Dear Donor Family,

"Thank you." We say it every day. Yet it's hard to find the words to thank you for the most precious gift of all—the gift of life.

Not a single day passes when I don't think of you, your pain and your humanity. Every day I try to live my life to the very fullest so I won't waste an ounce of your gift. I work, I exercise and I spend a lot of my free time working on the issue of organ donor awareness. I am young and—thanks to you—healthy.

I don't know you and yet you have taught me so much. Your family has profoundly changed my path. Your anonymous gift has allowed me to fall in love, travel to interesting places and greet my first nephew into the world. I hope knowing this will bring you some comfort. And I hope you can enjoy the fact that a part of your loved one lives on through me in this way.

May all your days get better and better. May we all find a reason in our hearts for the events that have forever linked our lives. With all my gratitude and best wishes,

A liver recipient

An Interview with
Rosemarie Hoferichter

After editing the manuscript of *The Waiting Game*, and as its publisher, I became intrigued with the life of the spouse of a transplant recipient, who is compelled to bravely carry on during the waiting game that spans so many months and often years before the transplant operation, hoping desperately for a donor's heart before it was too late. The wait becomes even more telling, knowing that some family will suffer untold grief at the loss of the loved one who will become the nameless donor, who's demise means so much to the life of the person their donation will save.

I tried to imagine the wait that becomes endless; for the match up of blood type of the right donor's organ; the special telephone call expected at anytime of the day or night, the hurried drive to the transplant hospital; parking and at last being able to reach into the trunk of the car to lift out that special piece of luggage packed months before; meeting the efficient medical staff and entrusting them with the care of the loved one; seeing the prone shape under the green sheet disappear behind a shiny door, then to suffer through the long wait and forever answering the question of making the right decision; and feeling the tears as prayers begin.

Time passes, each minute an hour of itself. The shiny door opens but it is not for you; again and again it is not for you; then the waiting game changes as the doctor walks toward you and you follow his every step with heart-stopping desperation, waiting for the sign and the comforting words that tell you of their success. The smile is slow in coming, its tired, but reassuring. There is a flood of relief.

I sought out Rosemarie Hoferichter, the wife of Bert Hoferichter the author, and suggested an interview. I knew he had spoken to her before as I had discussed the inclusion of a small piece about her that I would write for the book. She is very much part of his story-and very much a full partner in his life. After a pleasant drive to a town on Georgian Bay well known as a summer vacation spot, I met Bert and Rosemarie and followed them to their lovely home a few miles away. I knew of her prior reluctance to opening the door on her very private thoughts to an almost complete stranger, publisher of her husband's book or not. It was not something she felt compelled to do. Yet, being a devoted partner to the author of this book who was in favour of the idea, Rosemarie Hoferichter finally agreed.

We met under a colour-splashed patio umbrella with the author also sharing a deli lunch and a gentle-tasting bottle of German wine. The sun shone from a clear-blue sky adding to the warmth and conviviality.

Rosemarie is a tall, handsome, soft-spoken woman whose red hair is antithetical to her quiet persona, She spoke openly once we were left to ourselves, much if it being an affirmation of what had been written by her husband. I could understand her reserve, the holding within of herself that stemmed from an upbringing in a central Europe society. As we chatted, I could see and feel her quiet strength and realized more profoundly the terrifying test it had been put to during her husband's slow recovery from his major surgical procedure.

What I wanted to write about was the deep-set feelings that someone carries with themselves during such a trial. I was hoping to capture the essence of her life during this terrible life-threatening period so readers could feel what she had gone through. Her suffering was not as simple as if an accident had happened, with the shock of the policeman at the door, the rush to the bedside, then living through a disrupted life during the slow recovery to better health.

No, the waiting game is nothing like that. Rosemarie's days became a numbing wait, from the first visit to the hospital after the initial heart attack, to the final diagnosis often months and years later, that drugs and artery-clearing medical procedures were no longer capable of working their magic; that only another heart would do if her spouse was to survive.

But the day arrived, years later, when she waves to him from the front door as he leaves, smiling, to play his beloved game of golf. It is the first time in such a long arduous period that this was possible. She has a feeling of being blessed that it was able to happen.

Yet lurking, just below the surface, remains the anxiety, dormant, ready to emerge at the first unexpected telephone call when he is away from her.

I retain the memory of two people who love and respect each other. The aura of the pleasant visit stayed with me for days. Unfortunately the recording failed to allow me what I wanted—to be taken on the emotional roller-coaster ride that only a close family member can properly describe when a heart transplant operation and recovery becomes the only answer.

Bert Hoferichter said he couldn't have done it without Rosemarie. I had a brief glimpse into why that was true.

V. Wm. (Bill) Belfontaine
Abbeyfield Publishers

Organ Procurement Centres
in Canada

Below is a list of the organ procurement centres in Canada, with contact information.

Alberta:
H.O.P.E. Calgary. Foothill Hospital, 1404-29th Street NW., Calgary, Alberta T2N 2T9
Phone: (403) 283-2243

Alberta/Northwest Territories:
Human Organ Procurement Exchange,
Calgary: Phone: (403) 283-2243; Edmonton:
Phone: (403) 492-8411

British Columbia:
BC Transplant Society ,555 West 12th Avenue,
City Square, East Tower, 4th Floor, Vancouver, BC V5Z 3X7
Phone: (604) 877-2100

Manitoba:
Manitoba Transplant Program, Health Sciences Centre,
Room GE 441, 820 Sherbrook Street,
Winnipeg, Manitoba R3A 1R9
Phone: (204) 787-2071

New Brunswick:
Organ/Tissue Procurement Program, 8 Castle Street, P.O. Box 5001
Saint John, New Brunswick E2L 4Y9
Phone: (506) 787-2071

Newfoundland:
O.P.E.N. Program, Health Sciences Centre
2443 Prince Phillip Drive, St. John's, Newfoundland A1B 3V6
Phone: (709) 737-6600

Nova Scotia:
Multi-Organ Transplant Program, Queen Elizabeth
11 Health Sciences Centre, 1278 Tower Road,
Halifax, Nova Scotia B3H 2V9
Phone: (902) 473-5500

Ontario:
Transplant Ontario (formerly M.O.R.E. Ontario)
406-250 Dundas Street West, Toronto, Ontario M5T 2Z5
Phone: (416) 351-7328

Kingston Region
Kingston General Hospital, 76 Stuart Street,
Kingston, Ontario K7L 2V7
Phone: (613) 3232, ext. 4012

Multi-Organ Transplant Program, University Campus,
London Health Sciences Centre, 339 Windermere Road,
London, Ontario N6A 5A5
Phone: (519) 663-3060

Ottawa Region
Ottawa Civic Hospital, 1053 Carling Avenue,
Ottawa, Ontario K1Y 4E9
Phone: (613) 798-5555 ext. 7541

Ottawa General Hospital, 501 Smythe Road,
Ottawa, Ontario K1H 8L6
Phone: (613) 737-8616

Hamilton Region
St. Joseph's Hospital, 50 Charlton Avenue East,
Hamilton, Ontario L8N 1Y4
Phone: (905) 522-1155, ext. 3236

Multi-Organ Retrieval And Exchange Program,
Toronto General Hospital, General Division,
200 Elizabeth Street, Toronto, Ontario M5G 2C4
Phone: (416) 340-3587

Quebec:
Quebec Transplant, 1111-4200 rue St. Laurent,
Montreal, Quebec H2W 2R2
Phone: (514) 286-1414

Quebec Transplant, 2700 Jean Perrin, #212,
Quebec City, Quebec G2C 1S9
Phone: (418) 845-4110

Saskatchewan:
Saskatchewan Transplant Program, Royal University Hospital
103 Hospital Drive, P.O. Box 86,
Saskatoon, Saskatchewan S7N 0W8
Phone: (306) 966-1054

Donor and Donor Family
Consent Declaration Forms

The following are Donor and Donor Family consent forms. Please copy both pages, complete and store in a safe place.

DONOR CONSENT DECLARATION FORM

Name_____

In the hope I may help others, I am sharing my life by deciding to be an organ and tissue donor. Upon my death, I desire to donate:

      ☐ Any needed organs or tissues.
      ☐ Only the following organs or tissues:

Specify organ(s) or tissue(s).

_____

_____

_____

Signature of

Donor   _____

Next-of-Kin   _____

Relationship   _____

Date   _____

Please sign the statement and give it to the person (next of kin) most likely to be notified if you become involved in a medical emergency.

_____

_____

Transplant Ontario consent and declaration form

DONOR FAMILY CONSENT DECLARATION

This is to inform you that I want to be an organ and tissue donor, if the occasion ever arises. Please see that my wishes are carried out by informing attending medical personnel that I want to be a donor. This card is a heartfelt expression of my wishes.
Thank you.

Upon my death, I desire to donate:

❐ Any needed organs or tissues.
❐ Only the following organs or tissues:

Specify organ(s) or tissue(s).

_____

_____

_____

Signature of

Donor

_____

_____

_____

Next-of-Kin

Relationship

Date

_____

_____

_____

Transplant Ontario consent and declaration form

Useful Web Sites for Information

on

Organ Donation and Transplantation

or

General Health

The Internet offers an abundance of up-to-the-minute information on organ donation and transplantation from around the world. Here are a number of web sites that can be of help when looking for transplant or heart disease-related information.

U.S. RESOURCES

University of Michigan, Change of Heart Newsletter:
www.rjwitte.com/changeofheart

The United Network for Organ Sharing (UNOS):
www.unos.org

The New Health Thriveonline (the No. 1 consumer health site):
www.thriveonline.com

TransWeb:
www.transweb.org

Department of Health and Human Services (HRSA)
(U.S. government facts on transplantation and donation):
www.hrsa.gov

American Heart Association:
www.wmfrt.org

Heart Information Network:
www.heartinfo.org

Henry Ford Health System Transplantation:
www.hfhs.hapcorp.org

Research Corporation Technologies
(for research on new medication):
www.rctech.com

Cardiovascular Consultants Medical Group:
www.healthyhearts.com

HealthGate.com (for the latest health information):
www.bewell.com

Fitness Zone:
www.fitnesszone.com

The Summerfield Group
(for information on homocysteine and related products):
www.summerfieldgrop.com

Johns Hopkins University:
www.hopkins.med

University of Michigan:
www.umich.edu

RxList: The Internet Drug Index:
www.rxlist.com

Ask the Pharmacist:
www.wilmington.net/dees

Medscape Transplantation:
www.medscape.com

U.S. Health Watch:
www.healthwatch.com

American Society of Transplantation:
www.a-s-t.org

CANADIAN RESOURCES

The Canadian Association for Transplantation:
   www.transplant.ca

Canadian Organ Replacement Register (CORR):
   www.cihi.ca

Health Canada Online:
   www.hwc.ca

Ministry of Health Canada:
   www.gov.on.ca/health

Canadian Transplant Association (CTA):
   www.organ-donation-works.org

The Kidney Foundation of Canada:
   www.kidney.ca

Organ Donation Ontario, and Transplant Ontario:
(formerly the M.OR.E. Program)
   www.transplant-ontario.org

James McLaren's home page:
   http://pages.sprint.ca/transplantactivist/jamesmclaren.html

Norbert R.Hoferichter, Author's WebPages:
   www.organtransplantbook.com

British Columbia Transplant Society:
   www.transplant.bc.ca

London Health Science Centre:
   www.lhsc.on.ca/transplant

Multi-organ Transplant Program/Halifax Transplant Program:
   www.qez-hsc.ns.ca

University Health Network Transplant Unit/Toronto:
   www.transplantunite.org

Canadian Institute for Health Information:
   www.cihi.ca

EUROPEAN RESOURCES

Eurotransplant:
   www.transplant.org

International Transplant Coordinators Society:
   www.kuleuven.ac.be

Transplant Recipient International Organization:
   www.priment.com

World Health Organization:
   www.who.int

British Organ Donor Society:
   www.argonet.co.uk

Transplant Society of Australia and New Zealand:
   www.racp.edu.au

Transplant Patient Partnering Program:
   www.ktppp.com

The Transplant Sharing Exchange:
   www.ctstransplant.org

Collaborative Transplant Study:
   www.ctstransplant.org

Modern Miracles: Organ Transplants:
   www.library.thinkquest.org

Transplant Awareness Inc.:
   www.transplantawareness.org

Transplant Square:
   www.transplantsquare.com

Note: All URLs provided were correct upon publication. As the Web changes constantly, please search for more locations or links.

Glossary

angiogram	A radiographic-type technique whereby a substance is injected into a blood vessel for the purpose of identifying its anatomy by X-ray.
aneurysm	A localized dilation (ballooning outwards) of the wall of a blood vessel.
bank	A supply of human tissue or other materials, such as blood, skin, or sperm, held in reserve for future use.
brain death	Total cessation of brain function as manifested by the absence of consciousness, spontaneous movements, absence of respiration and of all brainstem functions. (Brainstem connection from brain to spine)
cadaveric	Referring to a dead body.

cornea	The clear tissue covering the front of the eyes, which allows light to enter.
coronary	Pertaining to encircling structures, as the coronary arteries.
creatine	An important nitrogenous compound produced by phosphorus.
critical care	Critical health care provided to a critically ill patient during a medical emergency or crisis.
cyclosporine	A fungal metabolite that has immunosuppressive properties. (Prevents rejection of transplanted organ.)
donor	The individual from whom the organ or tissue is removed, either living or cadaveric.
donor registry	A database of individuals who have given consent to become organ donors in the eventuality that they might become a candidate.
Digoxin	A cardiac glycoside obtained from leaves of Digitalis lanata. (For treatment of congestive heart failure and certain cardiac arrhythmia.)
diuretics	Drugs or substances tending to promote the formation and excretion of urine.
electroence phalogram	A diagnostic technique that measures the electrical activity of the brain, i.e., brain waves.
enema	A procedure in which a solution is introduced into the rectum for clearing clogged stool.
MRI test (Magnetic Resonance Imaging)	Medical imaging that uses nuclear magnetic resonance as its source of energy.

informed consent	The agreement of a person (or his or her legally authorized representative) to submit to any medical procedure, in full knowledge of all procedures and requirements as well as possible risks and benefits entailed.
intensive care	Advanced and highly specialized care provided to medical or surgical patients whose conditions are life-threatening and require comprehensive care.
organ	A group of tissues in a living organism that have been adapted to perform a specific function.
pancreas	The organ responsible for the production and secretion of insulin. (A gland that regulates fat and carbohydrates).
presumed consent	The system by which consent to donate is presumed unless a person has expressly indicated otherwise during his/her lifetime, the opting-out system.
procurement	The process of obtaining organs and tissues.
recipient	The individual who receives the donated tissue or organ.
regenerative	Having the capacity to regenerate, to produce anew.
registry	A place for registering, or a place where official records are kept.
rejection	Refers to the immunological process of sloughing off, or attacking, foreign tissue or an organ by the recipient organism.
renal	Having to do with the kidney.

required consent	The system by which persons wishing to donate organs or tissues must express their wishes during their lifetime, the opting-in system.
solid organs	These include the heart, lungs, kidneys, pancreas and liver.
tissue	A group of structurally and functionally similar cells and their intercellular material.
transplantation	Refers to a section of tissue or to a complete organ that is moved and implanted in another part of the body or in another body.
xeno-transplantation	The grafting of animal tissue or organs into human beings.

— • —

"Come work for the Lord.

The work is hard,

The hours are long,

And the pay is low,

But the retirement benefits are out of this world!"

— • —